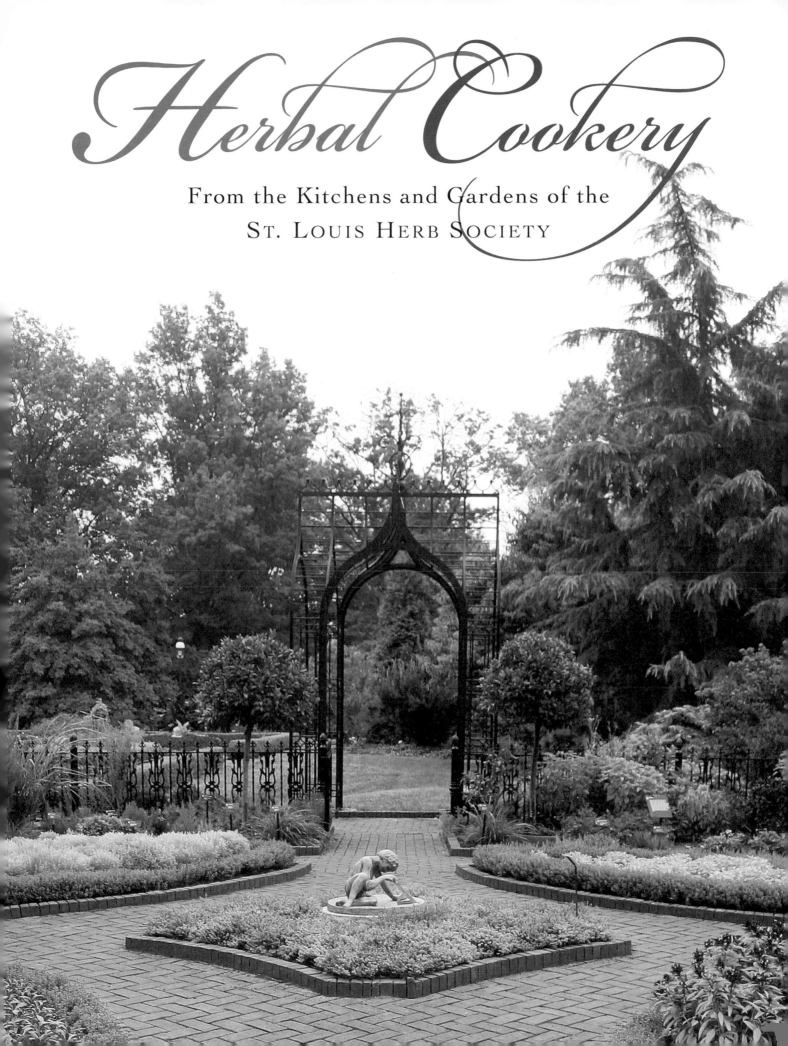

Herbal Cookery

From the Kitchens and Gardens of the
St. Louis Herb Society

Herbal Cookery

From the Kitchens and Gardens of the
ST. LOUIS HERB SOCIETY

Published by the St. Louis Herb Society

Copyright © 2009 by
THE ST. LOUIS HERB SOCIETY
www.stlouisherbsociety.org

Food Photography © Steve Adams
Garden Photography © THE ST. LOUIS HERB SOCIETY

Co-Chairs: Patricia Holt and Stephanie Prade

*This cookbook is a collection of favorite recipes,
which are not necessarily original recipes.*

Library of Congress Control Number: 2008909455

ISBN: 978-0-9643393-3-0

Edited, Designed, and Produced by

Favorite Recipes® Press
an imprint of

FRP®INC

a wholly owned subsidiary of Southwestern/Great American, Inc.
P. O. Box 305142
Nashville, Tennessee 37230
800-358-0560

Art Direction and Book Design: Starletta Polster
Project Editor: Linda A. Jones

Manufactured in the United States of America
First Printing: 2009
10,000 copies

Table of Contents

Appetizers & Beverages

Soups & Breads

Salads

Pastas & Grains

Vegetables 96

Meats 112

128

Poultry & Seafood

146

Desserts

Introduction

For more than sixty-five years, the St. Louis Herb Society has been dedicated to promoting the use and knowledge of herbs. Herbs bring richness and joy to one's life on many levels, but nowhere more delightfully than in the kitchen and the garden.

This cookbook, our fourth, is inspired by our belief that herbs, the useful plants, are to be enjoyed for both their magic in the kitchen and their beauty in the garden. As we plan and plant the St. Louis Herb Society Herb Garden with its six hundred different varieties and species of herbs, we are ever mindful of this, and as we continue to maintain this public herb garden at the Missouri Botanical Garden in St. Louis, Missouri, we are glad to share our knowledge and enthusiasm with you.

For thousands of years and in thousands of ways, herbs and spices have met the needs of mankind. It was not only useful but also necessary to season, spice, sweeten, and preserve food with the leaves, fruit, seeds, and, sometimes, roots of herbs. Today, nothing brings more pleasure to a meal than their addition to food. Whether fresh or dried, herbs bring seasonal variety to the art of cooking. No two versions of a recipe need ever be the same. This is the fun of herbal cookery.

Each spring and fall the St. Louis Herb Society conducts Adult Education Classes and hosts a Spring Herb Plant Sale Weekend at the Missouri Botanical Garden. Our Speakers Bureau provides speakers for community organizations. The St. Louis Herb Society also publishes *How to Grow Herbs in the Midwest* and *Lore and Legend of the Culinary Herbs and Spices*. They are both meant to be companions to this cookbook. We hope that *Herbal Cookery* will inspire you to grow herbs in your own garden and cook with them in your kitchen as we do in ours.

Beyond Herbaceous

Botanists define an herb as a small, seed-bearing plant with fleshy, or herbaceous parts rather than woody parts. But how does this describe a "bulb" of garlic? Fortunately, there is more than one way to classify a plant as an herb. A very broad description would be, "An herb is any useful plant." This definition suggests that spices are also herbs. To make the distinction between an herb and a spice, plant parts or climate zones are employed. Herbs usually grow in temperate zones and are the leafy part of plants, but other parts of the plant are also useful. Spices generally come from the bud, bark, rhizome, berry, seed, or flower stigma of plants grown in tropical zones. Overlapping does occur. For example, the herb cilantro produces brown seeds known as the spice coriander. Enjoy the abundant flavors of herbs and spices and use them frequently in your favorite recipes.

In times past, culinary herbs and spices were necessary to preserve foods and mask tainted odors and the taste of spoiled foods. Today herbs and spices are used to

- enhance or change the flavor of food;

- change the color or texture of food;

- create a signature dish to make it special; or

- substitute for a reduction in salt, sugar, or fat in a recipe.

Each herb and spice has its own unique makeup of plant chemicals known as phytochemicals. Phytochemicals protect plants from an array of damaging factors, such as radiation, fungus, and pests. They are also found in the "essential oils" of a plant, oils that give it a distinctive aroma and taste. These special substances impart their benefits to us when we consume them on a regular basis. Adding herbs and spices to a recipe not only enhances the taste of food but also contributes to good health.

Cocktail Party

Citrus Mint Vodka Martinis
38

Petite Beef Wellingtons with Dipping Sauces
24

Shrimp and Asparagus Dijonnaise in Puff Pastry
20

Stuffed Grape Leaves with Yogurt Sauce
27

Spiced Walnut and Three-Cheese Torta
33

Chai Meringues
157

Basil Orange Truffles
152

WINE SUGGESTIONS
Shiraz • Cabernet Sauvignon • Fumé Blanc • Sauvignon Blanc

Spring Brunch or Luncheon

Mai-Bowle
37

Wild Salmon Mousse
31

Meyer Lemon and Blueberry Soup
52

Garden Fresh Salad with Tomato Poppy Seed Dressing
70

Herb-Encrusted Rack of Lamb
120

White Asparagus with Lime Hollandaise Sauce
98

Cinnamon Rolls
65

Vanilla Bean Ice Cream with Lavender Syrup
164

LUNCHEON WINE SUGGESTIONS
Fumé Blanc • Merlot • Zinfandel

DESSERT WINE SUGGESTION
Riesling Kabinett

Tea Party

St. Louis Herb Society Tea-Pourri
37

Smoked Trout Mousse on Cucumber Slices
31

Avocado Deviled Eggs with Springtime Herbs
28

Lemon Cardamom Tea Bread
61

Rose Geranium Pound Cake
150

Fruit on Lemon Grass Skewers with Orange Tarragon Sauce
162

Lavender Blossom Tea Cookies
156

WINE SUGGESTIONS
Alsatian Riesling • Pinot Blanc • Grüner Veltliner

Spring Dinner Party

Lamb Meatballs with Cucumber Mint Sauce
26

Lemon Verbena Champagne Cocktail
37

Chilled Avocado Soup with Lemon Verbena and Sorrel
51

Veal and Herb–Stuffed Pasta with Béchamel Sauce
87

Green Beans with Amaretti Herb Crust
98

Cheddar Herb Knotted Rolls
64

Blackberry Basil Tart with Mascarpone Lemon Cream
160

APPETIZER WINE SUGGESTIONS
Côtes du Rhône • Pinot Grigio

DINNER WINE SUGGESTIONS
Chianti • Pinot Noir

DESSERT WINE SUGGESTION
Vin Santo

Cold Supper Alfresco for Two

Lobster Summer Rolls with Orange Ginger Mayonnaise
23

Grilled Chicories with Nasturtium Blossoms
71

Grilled Flank Steak and Cucumber Salad
79

Walnut Herb Bread
63

Lemon Mint Squares
154

APPETIZER WINE SUGGESTION
Champagne

SUPPER WINE SUGGESTION
Zinfandel

DESSERT WINE SUGGESTION
Moscatel

Barbecue Pool Party

Shrimp from the Outer Banks
21

Pineapple Salsa
35

Mahimahi Tacos with Avocado Mango Salsa
136

Apple Cheeseburgers with Lemon Horseradish Mousse
118

Basil Corn Salad with Green Beans and Cherry Tomatoes
72

Focaccia with Brushed Herb Topping
62

Chocolate Chipotle Brownies
153

Orange Basil Sandwich Cookies
157

APPETIZER WINE AND BEER SUGGESTIONS
Champagne • Sauvignon Blanc • Spring beer with lemon and herbal notes

DINNER WINE AND BEER SUGGESTIONS
Shiraz • India Pale Ale • Primitivo

Autumn Harvest Dinner

Herbed Pistachio Pâté with Gala Apples
32

Corn Chowder with White Wine and Herbs
46

Grilled Pork Tenderloin with Port Cranberry Sauce
123

Balsamic-Glazed Harvest Vegetables
110

Chive Biscuits
58

Pear and Pecan Upside-Down Cake with Maple Cream
148

APPETIZER WINE SUGGESTIONS
Oaked Chardonnay • Gewürztraminer

DINNER WINE SUGGESTIONS
Shiraz • Zinfandel

DESSERT WINE SUGGESTION
Late Harvest Riesling

Christmas Dinner

Miniature Crab Cakes
22

Gala Apple and Pear Salad with Mustard Pear Vinaigrette
69

Peppered Roast Beef Tenderloin with Garlic Oregano Sauce
115

Cranberry Wild Rice with Peas
94

Spinach Gratin
105

Basil Popovers with Garlic Chive Butter
56

Cranberry Rosemary Meringue Pie
158

APPETIZER WINE SUGGESTIONS
Pinot Grigio   •   Sauvignon Blanc

DINNER WINE SUGGESTION
Barolo

DESSERT WINE SUGGESTION
Brachetto d'Acqui

Appetizers & Beverages

Shrimp and Asparagus Dijonnaise in Puff Pastry, page 20

Shrimp and Asparagus Dijonnaise in Puff Pastry

DIJONNAISE DRESSING
1/3 cup mayonnaise
2 tablespoons Dijon mustard
1/2 teaspoon lemon zest
1/2 teaspoon lemon juice

APPETIZERS
18 asparagus spears, trimmed
1 (17-ounce) package frozen puff pastry sheets,
     or 18 cocktail phyllo shells
18 shrimp, cooked and peeled
2 teaspoons chopped fresh citrus mint leaves,
     such as lemon or orange

EQUIPMENT NEEDED: A large skillet with lid; baking parchment; a miniature muffin pan

To prepare the dressing, combine the mayonnaise, Dijon mustard, lemon zest and lemon juice in a small bowl and mix well.

To prepare the appetizers, place the asparagus in a large skillet and cover with cold water. Bring to a boil and remove from the heat. Let stand, covered, for 3 minutes. Drain and rinse with cold water. Drain and pat dry. Cut off the tips and reserve for garnish. Cut the remaining spears into 1/4-inch pieces and place in a bowl. Add the dressing and toss to coat. Chill, covered, until ready to use.

Thaw the pastry for 30 minutes. Roll one pastry sheet into a 71/2×15-inch rectangle on a lightly floured sheet of baking parchment. Cut out nine 21/2-inch circles. Repeat with the remaining pastry sheet. (The pastry rounds may be frozen on a baking sheet at this point and stored in a sealable plastic freezer bag until ready to use. Thaw and continue with the recipe.)

Preheat the oven to 400 degrees. Press the pastry rounds into ungreased miniature muffin cups. Bake for 10 minutes or until golden brown, watching carefully to prevent overbrowning. Remove from the oven and tap down the centers while hot to form a shell. Let stand until cool. Spoon 1 teaspoon of the asparagus mixture into each shell. Place a reserved asparagus tip straight up in each and wrap with a shrimp. Sprinkle with the mint. Serve immediately or chill until serving time.

Note: These delectable and elegant little appetizers can be prepared the day before and assembled at the last minute. Our method for blanching asparagus is perfect every time.

 ## Keeping Fresh Herbs Handy

Keep a small bouquet of fresh, stemmed herbs in a vase of fresh water on your kitchen counter while you are cooking. Not only does it brighten the kitchen, but it fills your home with the satisfying scent of herbs. You may also wash and pat the herbs dry, wrap in a paper towel to absorb moisture, then place in a sealable plastic bag and chill. The herbs should stay fresh for several days. Keep a glass of fresh herbs in the refrigerator to keep odors away, in place of the customary box of baking soda.

Shrimp from the Outer Banks

3 onions, thinly sliced
1 red bell pepper, sliced into 1/4-inch strips
1 pound mushrooms, sliced
4 garlic cloves, flattened with a knife
1 1/2 cups red wine vinegar
3/4 cup vegetable oil
3/4 cup extra-virgin olive oil
3 tablespoons sugar
6 tablespoons capers with juice

2 fresh bay leaves
3 tablespoons chopped fresh tarragon leaves
1 tablespoon fennel seeds
2 teaspoons celery seeds
2 teaspoons salt
1 or 2 dashes of Tabasco Sauce
2 pounds large (21- to 30-count) shrimp,
    peeled and deveined

EQUIPMENT NEEDED: A large saucepan

Combine the onions, bell pepper, mushrooms, garlic, vinegar, vegetable oil, olive oil, sugar, capers, bay leaves, tarragon, fennel seeds, celery seeds, salt and Tabasco sauce in a large glass bowl to make a marinade. Mix well. Cook the shrimp in boiling water in a large saucepan for 2 minutes or until the shrimp turn pink. Drain well. Add the hot shrimp to the vegetable mixture and toss to coat. Chill, covered, for 24 hours or longer, stirring occasionally.

To serve, remove the garlic cloves and bay leaves from the shrimp mixture. Remove the shrimp and vegetables from the marinade with a slotted spoon and arrange on individual serving plates as a first course. Or, serve the drained shrimp mixture in a glass bowl and provide tongs for guests to serve themselves.

Note: The inspiration for this recipe came from the area around Nags Head, North Carolina, known as the Outer Banks. If you prefer a more tart marinade, you may reduce the amount of sugar, but we believe we have found the perfect balance between sweet and tart.

Crab and Avocado Cocktail

2 ripe avocados, chopped
1 tablespoon lime juice
2 tablespoons sour cream
1 tablespoon lemon juice
1 tablespoon finely chopped fresh cilantro

Salt and freshly ground pepper to taste
1 cup cooked fresh crab meat
3 tablespoons unsweetened coconut milk
1/2 teaspoon finely grated fresh gingerroot
Chopped fresh flat-leaf parsley for garnish

EQUIPMENT NEEDED: 8 martini glasses; 8 small spoons

Make certain all ingredients are chilled before beginning the recipe. Toss the avocados with the lime juice in a bowl. Reserve one-half of the avocados and set aside. Mash the remaining avocados with the sour cream, lemon juice, cilantro, salt and pepper. Combine the crab meat, coconut milk and gingerroot in a bowl and mix gently. Season with salt and pepper. Divide the avocado mixture equally among eight martini glasses. Divide the crab mixture into eight portions and spoon over the avocado mixture. Top with the reserved avocados. Garnish with parsley. Serve immediately and provide small spoons.

Note: Avocados should be ripe, but not too soft.

Miniature Crab Cakes

3 tablespoons unsalted butter
1/2 small onion, finely chopped
1/2 red bell pepper, finely chopped
1/2 rib celery, finely chopped
2 garlic cloves, minced
1 pound crab meat, shells removed and
  meat flaked
1 egg
1/4 cup mayonnaise
1/2 cup panko (Japanese bread crumbs)

1 tablespoon finely chopped fresh
  flat-leaf parsley
3/4 teaspoon Seafood Seasoning Mix
  (recipe follows) or store-bought equivalent
1/4 teaspoon cayenne pepper
2 tablespoons prepared mustard
1 teaspoon Worcestershire sauce
1/2 teaspoon fresh lemon juice
All-purpose flour for dusting
Olive oil for frying

EQUIPMENT NEEDED: A 10-inch skillet; a baking sheet

Melt the butter in a 10-inch skillet over medium heat. Add the onion, bell pepper, celery and garlic and sauté for 2 minutes. Remove from the heat to cool. Combine the cooled vegetables, crab meat, egg, mayonnaise, panko, parsley, seasoning mix, cayenne pepper, mustard, Worcestershire sauce and lemon juice in a large bowl and mix well. Shape into twenty-four patties and place on a baking sheet. Chill for 1 hour to allow the flavors to meld. (The patties can be frozen at this point.) Dust the patties with flour. Fry in olive oil in a 10-inch skillet over medium heat until golden brown on each side. Serve with fresh salsa or favorite condiments.

Note: The best crab cakes are chilled before cooking to prevent falling apart. The patties may be broiled instead of fried.

Seafood Seasoning Mix

2 tablespoons ground bay leaves
2 tablespoons celery salt
1 tablespoon dry mustard
2 teaspoons black pepper
2 teaspoons ginger
2 teaspoons sweet paprika
1 teaspoon white pepper

1 teaspoon nutmeg
1 teaspoon ground cloves
1 teaspoon ground allspice
1/2 teaspoon crushed red pepper flakes
1/2 teaspoon ground mace
1/2 teaspoon ground cardamom
1/2 teaspoon dried lemon zest

EQUIPMENT NEEDED: An airtight container

Combine the bay leaves, celery salt, dry mustard, black pepper, ginger, paprika, white pepper, nutmeg, cloves, allspice, red pepper flakes, mace, cardamom and lemon zest in a bowl and mix well. Store in an airtight container.

 ## Mustard

The ground black, white, or brown seeds of the genus *Brassica* form the base of what we call "mustard." American, ballpark-style yellow mustard is made with white seeds. Dijon mustard is made from husked black seeds. English mustard is made with white seeds. German mustard is a smooth blend of vinegar and black seeds and varies in heat. East Indian dishes use brown seeds that have been pounded into a paste or an oil extract.

Lobster Summer Rolls with Orange Ginger Mayonnaise

ORANGE GINGER MAYONNAISE
1 cup mayonnaise
Zest and juice of 1 orange
1 teaspoon minced fresh gingerroot

ROLLS
12 rice paper spring roll wrappers
8 ounces cooked lobster meat
1 mango, sliced
1 avocado, sliced
1/2 cup shredded carrots
1/2 cup shredded daikon
1/2 bunch fresh cilantro, chopped
12 fresh shiso or basil leaves, chiffonade cut
Fresh cilantro for garnish

EQUIPMENT NEEDED: Any wide, shallow pan

To prepare the ginger mayonnaise, combine the mayonnaise, orange zest, orange juice and gingerroot in a bowl and mix well.

To prepare the rolls, soak one wrapper at a time in warm water in a wide, shallow pan until softened. Remove from the water and place smooth side down on a lint-free towel to drain the excess water. Spread a spoonful of the mayonnaise across the bottom third of the wrapper, leaving a 1-inch margin on the sides and bottom. Layer the lobster meat, mango, avocado, carrots, daikon, chopped cilantro and shiso over the mayonnaise layer to create a filling 1 inch thick. Roll tightly to enclose the filling, folding in the sides as you roll. Repeat with the remaining wrappers, mayonnaise and filling.

To serve, cut each roll diagonally into halves. Garnish with cilantro.

Note: Meaning "large root," the daikon is shaped like a large carrot, but it is actually a large, white radish. Also known as Oriental radish, its flavor is crisp and mild.

Petite Beef Wellingtons with Dipping Sauces

1 (1-pound) beef tenderloin, cut into
  36 (3/4-inch) cubes
1/2 teaspoon salt
1 teaspoon freshly ground pepper
1 tablespoon minced garlic
1 tablespoon chopped fresh thyme
1 (17-ounce) package frozen puff pastry
  sheets, thawed
1 tablespoon stone-ground mustard with
  bourbon whiskey

1 tablespoon prepared horseradish
9 slices smoked Gouda cheese,
  cut into quarters
1 medium egg, beaten
Sour Cream and Horseradish Dipping Sauce
  (recipe page 25)
Raisin and Currant Dipping Sauce
  (recipe page 25)

EQUIPMENT NEEDED: A large baking sheet; baking parchment

Spread the beef cubes on a large baking sheet and sprinkle with the salt, pepper, garlic and thyme. Freeze until firm. Place in a sealable freezer bag. Store in the freezer until ready to use.

Roll one pastry sheet into a 15×15-inch rectangle on a lightly floured sheet of baking parchment. Cut into eighteen squares. Repeat with the remaining pastry sheet. Mix the mustard and horseradish in a bowl. Place a frozen beef cube in the center of each pastry square. Place a cheese quarter over the beef and top with a tiny dab of the mustard mixture. Fold the sides of the pastry up and over the filling to form an envelope and seal to enclose the filling.

Preheat the oven to 400 degrees. Place the parcels folded side up on a baking sheet lined with baking parchment. Make a small slit in the top of each to allow the steam to escape. Brush with the egg. Bake for 20 minutes or until crisp and golden brown. Remove from the baking sheet immediately. Serve hot with the dipping sauces.

Note: These little parcels made with the finest beef are best served straight from the oven. They can be prepared in advance, frozen, and then baked the day of your party. For extra flavor, sprinkle thyme, garlic, and shallots on the pastry dough before adding the beef.

Variation: Omit the mustard, horseradish and Gouda cheese and use 12 ounces blue cheese or 8 ounces softened coarse pâté.

Sour Cream and Horseradish Dipping Sauce

^{1}/2 cup sour cream
^{1}/2 cup mayonnaise
3 tablespoons prepared horseradish

^{1}/4 teaspoon salt
1^1/4 teaspoons freshly ground pepper

Combine the sour cream, mayonnaise, horseradish, salt and pepper in a small bowl and mix well. Store, covered, in the refrigerator until serving time.

Raisin and Currant Sauce

^{1}/4 cup (^{1}/2 stick) butter
^{1}/2 cup packed brown sugar
2 tablespoons cornstarch
^{1}/4 cup orange juice

1^1/2 cups apple cider
^{1}/4 cup raisins
1 tablespoon currant jelly
1^1/2 teaspoons ground allspice

EQUIPMENT NEEDED: A small saucepan

Melt the butter with the brown sugar in a small saucepan. Mix the cornstarch and orange juice together in a small bowl and add to the brown sugar mixture. Stir in the apple cider, raisins, jelly and allspice. Heat until the brown sugar is completely dissolved and the sauce is thickened, stirring constantly.

Note: The sauce may be frozen.

 Freezing Herbs

Parsley, sage, rosemary, and thyme all freeze well. Pick them in the morning when the sun has brought up the herbs' essential oils. Wash, pat dry, and then strip the leaves from the stems. Place the leaves on a baking sheet lined with waxed paper or baking parchment. Freeze for four hours, then place them in sealable plastic freezer bags and seal tightly. Be certain to date and label them. Frozen herbs are best if used within three months.

Lamb Meatballs with Cucumber Mint Sauce

CUCUMBER MINT SAUCE
12 ounces Greek strained yogurt
1 cup coarsely grated peeled cucumber
1/4 cup chopped fresh cilantro
1/4 cup chopped fresh mint leaves
1 tablespoon fresh lime juice
1/2 teaspoon salt

MEATBALLS
1 1/2 teaspoons olive oil
1/2 cup minced yellow onion
1 large garlic clove, minced

1 pound ground lamb
1/2 cup fine fresh bread crumbs
1 egg, lightly beaten
1 tablespoon finely chopped fresh cilantro
1 tablespoon finely chopped fresh mint leaves
1/2 teaspoon ground cumin
1/4 teaspoon ground allspice
1/4 teaspoon cinnamon
1/4 teaspoon nutmeg
1 teaspoon salt
1/8 teaspoon freshly ground pepper

EQUIPMENT NEEDED: A small skillet; a 10×15-inch baking pan

To prepare the sauce, combine the yogurt, cucumber, cilantro, mint, lime juice and salt in a bowl and mix well. Chill, covered, for 2 to 3 hours to allow the flavors to meld.

To prepare the meatballs, heat the olive oil in a small skillet over medium heat. Add the onion and garlic and sauté until softened. Remove from the heat to cool slightly. Combine the onion mixture, lamb, bread crumbs, egg, cilantro, mint, cumin, allspice, cinnamon, nutmeg, salt and pepper in a large bowl and mix well. Shape into 1-inch meatballs and place in a bowl. Chill, covered, in the refrigerator. (The meatballs can be made up to 1 day in advance up to this point.)

Preheat the oven to 450 degrees. Place the meatballs in a single layer in a greased 10×15-inch baking pan. Place in the oven and reduce the oven temperature to 350 degrees. Bake for 20 minutes or until light brown and cooked through. Serve with the sauce.

Note: Do not overcook these meatballs. They should be moist and succulent.

Storing and Using Dried Herbs

Store dried herbs in a cool, dry, dark place away from the stove and refrigerator. Dried herbs begin to lose potency after six months, so buy small quantities of seldom-used herbs. If possible, purchase and store dried herbs in the whole-leaf form. When ready to use, crush the leaves in the palm of your hand. The heat from your hands will release the essential oils to bring out the fragrance in the herbs. Burn old herbs in your fireplace or outdoor grill for a burst of woodsy aroma.

Stuffed Grape Leaves with Yogurt Sauce

YOGURT SAUCE
1 cup Greek strained yogurt
1/2 teaspoon pressed garlic
   (about 2 small cloves)
1/2 teaspoon paprika
Chopped fresh flat-leaf parsley for garnish
Chopped fresh chives for garnish

STUFFED GRAPE LEAVES
1 (8-ounce) jar grape leaves
1/2 cup pine nuts
1 tablespoon olive oil
1/4 teaspoon salt
1 1/2 cups chopped yellow onions

2 tablespoons olive oil
2/3 cup golden raisins
2 teaspoons ground cumin
1 cup long-grain white rice
1 teaspoon salt
1 teaspoon freshly ground pepper
1 1/2 cups vegetable broth
3 tablespoons chopped fresh chives
3 tablespoons chopped fresh oregano
3 tablespoons chopped fresh flat-leaf parsley
1 cup vegetable broth
Lemon juice for sprinkling
Lemon wedges for garnish

EQUIPMENT NEEDED: A large saucepan; a medium skillet with lid; a 9×13-inch glass or ceramic baking dish

To prepare the sauce, combine the yogurt, garlic and paprika in a small bowl and mix well. Spoon into a serving bowl and garnish with parsley and chives. Chill, covered, until serving time.

To prepare the stuffed grape leaves, blanch the grape leaves in boiling water in a large saucepan for 30 seconds. Plunge immediately into cold water to stop the cooking process. Remove the leaves from the water using a slotted spoon and place on paper towels or linen towels to drain. Pat dry and cut off any protruding stems with kitchen scissors.

Sauté the pine nuts in 1 tablespoon olive oil in a medium skillet until light brown, being careful not to burn. Remove from the skillet and sprinkle with 1/4 teaspoon salt. Let stand until cool. Sauté the onions in 2 tablespoons olive oil in the skillet over medium heat until golden brown. Stir in the raisins and cumin. Add the rice, 1 teaspoon salt, the pepper and 1 1/2 cups broth and mix well. Bring to a boil; reduce the heat. Simmer, covered, for 10 minutes or until the rice is partially cooked and the liquid is absorbed, stirring occasionally. Let cool to lukewarm. Stir in the chives, oregano, parsley and pine nuts.

Preheat the oven to 375 degrees. Place a grape leaf vein side up on a flat surface. Spoon 1 1/2 to 2 tablespoons of the rice mixture in the center of the widest part of the leaf. Fold the bottom part of the leaf over the filling. Fold in the sides and roll up tightly. Repeat with the remaining grape leaves and filling. Arrange seam side down in a tight single layer in a greased 9×13-inch glass or ceramic baking dish. Pour 1 cup broth over the top. Bake, covered tightly with foil, for 45 minutes or until the rice is tender. Sprinkle with lemon juice just before serving and garnish with lemon wedges. Serve warm or cold with the sauce.

Note: Blanching the grape leaves rids the leaves of their packing brine and makes them easier to handle. Our Yogurt Sauce must be made with Greek yogurt, a thick, rich, and creamy yogurt that has already been strained. Any substitute will only disappoint. This dish can be made one day in advance, cooled slightly, and stored, covered, in the refrigerator until serving time.

Avocado Deviled Eggs with Springtime Herbs

1 dozen small or medium eggs
Salt to taste
1/2 teaspoon St. Louis Herb Society Curry
    Powder (page 49) or store-bought equivalent
2 tablespoons (heaping) mayonnaise or more
1/2 ripe avocado, chopped
1 tablespoon (heaping) mayonnaise

1 tablespoon mayonnaise-type salad dressing
Chopped fresh herbs, such as dill, parsley,
    tarragon or thyme for garnish
2 or 3 black olives, very thinly sliced
    for garnish
2 or 3 grape tomatoes, very thinly sliced
    for garnish

EQUIPMENT NEEDED: A large saucepan

Place the eggs in a large saucepan and cover with salted water. Bring to a boil; remove from the heat. Cover and let stand for 15 minutes. Drain and rinse with cold water to stop the cooking process. Let stand until cool. Peel the eggs. Cut a small slice off of both ends of the eggs so each egg half will stand upright. Cut each egg into halves crosswise (not lengthwise). Remove the yolks from sixteen of the egg halves and place in a bowl. Add the curry powder, 2 heaping tablespoons mayonnaise and salt. Mash with a fork until smooth, adding additional mayonnaise if needed. Pipe or spoon into twelve egg white halves. Mash the remaining eight egg yolk halves, the avocado, 1 heaping tablespoon mayonnaise, the salad dressing and salt in a small bowl until smooth. Pipe or spoon into the remaining egg white halves. Decorate the tops with a combination of fresh herbs, olive slices and tomato slices.

Note: Our deviled eggs are the colors of spring, a combination of yellow and green. For even more color, line the serving plate with purple cabbage. Deviled eggs should be moist, but not runny, and smooth without lumps. For the best consistency, force the yolks through a fine sieve. Older eggs are easier to peel.

Caprese Kabobs on Rosemary Sprigs

ROSEMARY VINAIGRETTE
1/4 cup red wine vinegar
1 tablespoon chopped fresh rosemary
1 teaspoon sugar
1/2 teaspoon salt
1/4 teaspoon freshly ground pepper
Dash of Tabasco sauce
3/4 cup extra-virgin olive oil

KABOBS
8 to 10 firm sprigs of fresh rosemary,
    leaves stripped (reserve the leaves for
    the vinaigrette)
22 grape tomatoes
22 small fresh basil leaves
1 (12-ounce) container bite-size mozzarella
    balls marinated in olive oil with herbs

To prepare the vinaigrette, combine the vinegar, rosemary, sugar, salt, pepper and Tabasco sauce in a bowl. Drizzle in the olive oil, whisking constantly until emulsified.

To prepare the kabobs, cut the rosemary sprigs into 3-inch lengths. Place the tomatoes in a sealable plastic bag and add the vinaigrette. Seal the bag and marinate for 30 minutes or longer. Drain the tomatoes, reserving the vinaigrette. Skewer one tomato, one basil leaf and one mozzarella ball onto each rosemary sprig. Drizzle each with a few drops of the reserved vinaigrette.

Note: Make these kabobs when the stems of your rosemary are as firm as wooden picks.

Rosemary (*Rosmarinus officinalis*)

Endive with Apple, Cheeses and Almonds

3¹/₂ ounces crumbled blue cheese
1¹/₂ cups whole milk ricotta cheese
1 large tart red apple, such as Gala
1 tablespoon fresh lemon juice
³/₄ cup finely chopped celery
1 teaspoon finely chopped shallot
2 tablespoons minced fresh chives
2 tablespoons minced fresh flat-leaf parsley
1 tablespoon chopped fresh tarragon

¹/₄ teaspoon salt
3 tablespoons mayonnaise
¹/₂ cup honey-roasted almonds,
   coarsely chopped
5 heads of Belgian endive
Chopped fresh tarragon for garnish
¹/₄ cup honey-roasted almonds, coarsely
   chopped for garnish

Mix the blue cheese and ricotta cheese in a small bowl and set aside. Core the apple and cut into ¹/₈-inch pieces. Place in a bowl and sprinkle with the lemon juice. Combine the celery, shallot, chives, parsley, 1 tablespoon tarragon, the salt and mayonnaise in a bowl and mix well. Stir in the apple and ¹/₂ cup almonds.

Cut off the ends of the endive and separate the leaves. Arrange the leaves on a serving plate. Top each with a dollop of the cheese mixture and a spoonful of the apple mixture. Garnish with chopped tarragon and ¹/₄ cup almonds. Serve chilled or at room temperature.

Note: Endive becomes more bitter as it is exposed to light, so buy the freshest available, preferably one that has been wrapped. A member of the chicory family, endive is grown completely underground.

 ## How Much to Use

Although personal taste determines how much of an individual herb or combination of herbs is used to flavor any recipe, it is wise to start cautiously. Many herb cooks suggest that with mild to medium herbs, start with a teaspoon of chopped fresh herbs or one-half teaspoon dried herbs in dishes that serve four. Use half that amount with stronger herbs.

Smoked Trout Mousse on Cucumber Slices   MAKES 36 TO 40 ROUNDS

8 ounces cream cheese, softened
6 ounces goat cheese, softened
8 ounces smoked trout, skin and bones
  removed and trout flaked
1/3 cup finely chopped fresh chives
3 tablespoons finely chopped fresh dill

2 tablespoons finely chopped fresh
  flat-leaf parsley
1 tablespoon chopped scallions (white part only)
3 cucumbers (about 8 ounces each)
Salad burnet, sprigs of dill, chopped fresh
  chives or chive blossoms for garnish

EQUIPMENT NEEDED: A colander

Beat the cream cheese and goat cheese in a medium bowl until smooth. Stir in the trout, 1/3 cup chives, 3 tablespoons dill, the parsley and scallions. Chill the mousse, covered, for 2 hours or longer.

Peel the cucumbers and cut into 1/2-inch slices. Place in a colander and drain for 15 minutes or longer. Place the cucumbers on a paper towel and cover with another paper towel. Press lightly to dry. Wrap the cucumbers in paper towels and store in the refrigerator until serving time. (Drying will prevent the mousse from sliding off the cucumber slices.)

To serve, shape a generous teaspoonful of the mousse at a time into a ball. Place each in the center of a cucumber slice and flatten slightly. Garnish with salad burnet, sprigs of dill, chopped chives or chive blossoms. Serve chilled.

Note: When your garden chives are in bloom, the blossoms of purple and white make an exquisite garnish for this crisp and refreshing appetizer.

Wild Salmon Mousse   SERVES 10 TO 12

1 envelope unflavored gelatin
1/2 cup warm water
2 pounds cooked wild salmon
1 garlic clove, chopped
8 ounces cream cheese, softened
8 ounces whole milk ricotta cheese
1/2 cup sour cream

1/2 cup mayonnaise
1/3 cup lemon juice
1 teaspoon salt
1 teaspoon chopped fresh mint leaves
1/2 teaspoon chopped fresh lemon thyme
1/2 teaspoon paprika
Tabasco sauce to taste

EQUIPMENT NEEDED: A food processor; a decorative 5-cup mold

Soften the gelatin in a small amount of cold water in a bowl. Stir in the warm water and set aside. Purée the salmon, garlic, cream cheese, ricotta cheese, sour cream, mayonnaise, lemon juice, salt, mint, lemon thyme, paprika and Tabasco sauce in a food processor. Add the gelatin mixture and pulse to combine. Pour into a decorative 5-cup mold. Chill for 8 to 10 hours or until set. Unmold onto a serving plate and serve with toasted pumpernickel bread fingers.

Note: A dense pumpernickel bread with whole rye berries is a must for this creamy mousse.

Herbed Pistachio Pâté with Gala Apples

1 pound chicken livers
1 yellow onion, coarsely chopped
1 tablespoon pressed garlic
1 large bay leaf
1 tablespoon fresh thyme leaves
1 1/2 tablespoons fresh rosemary leaves
1/2 teaspoon salt
1 cup chicken broth (preferably homemade)
3/4 cup (1 1/2 sticks) unsalted butter, softened
3 tablespoons brandy or Cognac

1/4 teaspoon fresh rosemary leaves
1/4 teaspoon ginger
1/4 teaspoon nutmeg
1 teaspoon salt
1/2 teaspoon freshly ground pepper
1 cup roasted pistachios, coarsely chopped
1 cup heavy whipping cream
Sliced Gala apples
Black bread or toast points

EQUIPMENT NEEDED: A medium saucepan; a food processor or blender; a hand mixer; a 3-cup decorative serving dish

Combine the chicken livers, onion, garlic, bay leaf, thyme, 1 1/2 tablespoons rosemary, 1/2 teaspoon salt and the broth in a medium saucepan. Bring to a boil. Reduce the heat and simmer, covered, for 6 to 8 minutes or until the chicken livers are light pink in the center, turning the chicken livers a few times. Remove from the heat. Let cool for 20 minutes to infuse the chicken livers with the herb flavors.

Drain the chicken livers, discarding the bay leaf. Process the chicken livers, butter, brandy, 1/4 teaspoon rosemary, the ginger, nutmeg, 1 teaspoon salt and the pepper in a food processor or blender until smooth, stopping to scrape down the side frequently. Spoon into a medium bowl. Stir in the pistachios. Chill, covered, for 20 minutes or until thoroughly chilled.

Whip the cream in a mixing bowl with a hand mixer until stiff peaks form. Fold into the chilled purée. Pack into a 3-cup decorative serving dish. Chill, covered, for at least 24 hours or up to 48 hours before serving. Serve with apple slices and black bread or toast points.

Note: Our pâté is smooth and creamy, yet crunchy. It can double as an appetizer or a first course. As a first course, pack the pâté into individual ramekins lined with cheesecloth and chill. Just before serving, unmold onto a bed of Bibb lettuce and surround with apple slices and black bread or toast points.

Spiced Walnut and Three-Cheese Torta

SERVES 20

1 large garlic clove, pressed
1/3 cup sugar
1 teaspoon chili powder
1/2 teaspoon cayenne pepper
1/2 teaspoon ground cumin
1/2 teaspoon salt
1 cup water
1 cup walnuts
8 ounces good-quality blue cheese, crumbled
8 ounces cream cheese, softened

5 ounces goat cheese such as Montrachet
1/4 cup (1/2 stick) unsalted butter, softened
1/3 cup chopped scallions (white parts only)
3 tablespoons brandy
1/2 cup finely chopped fresh basil leaves
1/4 cup finely chopped fresh flat-leaf parsley
Walnuts for garnish
Chopped scallion tops for garnish
Chopped fresh basil leaves for garnish
Chopped fresh flat-leaf parsley for garnish

EQUIPMENT NEEDED: A small saucepan; a baking sheet; a 4-cup mold or loaf pan

Combine the garlic, sugar, chili powder, cayenne pepper, cumin, salt and water in a small saucepan and mix well. Cook over high heat to 235 degrees on a candy thermometer, soft-ball stage. Remove from the heat. Add 1 cup walnuts and stir until coated. Place on a greased baking sheet and separate to cool. Chop coarsely and set aside.

Combine one-half of the blue cheese, the cream cheese, goat cheese and butter in a small bowl and mix until smooth. Stir in the scallions and brandy and set aside. Mix 1/2 cup basil and 1/4 cup parsley in a small bowl and set aside.

Lightly grease a 4-cup mold or loaf pan. Line with plastic wrap so that the plastic extends generously over the edges. Spread one-third of the cheese mixture evenly in the bottom of the mold. Press one-half of the walnuts into the cheese layer. Scatter one-half of the remaining blue cheese over the walnut layer. Sprinkle one-half of the herb mixture over the blue cheese layer. Repeat the layers with one-half of the remaining cheese mixture, the remaining walnuts, remaining blue cheese and remaining herb mixture. Top with the remaining cheese mixture. Press the layers down with the back of a spoon. Fold the plastic wrap over the top to cover completely. Chill for 8 to 10 hours.

To serve, unfold the plastic wrap from the top of the torta and invert onto a serving platter. Remove the pan and plastic wrap. Garnish with walnuts, scallion tops, basil and parsley.

Corn and Avocado Salsa

2 tablespoons extra-virgin olive oil
4 cups fresh corn kernels
 (from about 4 large ears)
1 large red onion, chopped
1 large red bell pepper, chopped
1/2 cup pitted green or black olives,
 chopped (optional)
2 garlic cloves, minced

Juice of 2 limes
3 tablespoons Red Wine Ravigote Vinegar
 (recipe follows) or other red wine vinegar
1/3 cup extra-virgin olive oil
1/3 cup chopped fresh cilantro, or 2 tablespoons
 chopped fresh oregano
Salt and freshly ground pepper to taste
2 ripe avocados, cut into 1/2-inch chunks

EQUIPMENT NEEDED: A 14-inch skillet

Heat 2 tablespoons olive oil in a 14-inch skillet over medium-high heat until shimmering. Add the corn and cook until some of the kernels are brown and slightly dry. Combine the corn, onion, bell pepper, olives, garlic, lime juice, vinegar, 1/3 cup olive oil, the cilantro, salt and pepper in a medium bowl and mix well. Marinate at room temperature for a few hours. Fold in the avocados just before serving.

Note: Use as a salsa with chips, or serve over a bed of lettuce with sliced or wedge-cut tomatoes.

Red Wine Ravigote Vinegar

1 quart (4 cups) red wine vinegar
2 cups fresh salad burnet
1 cup fresh basil
1 cup fresh tarragon

1/2 cup fresh thyme
1 hot red chile
1 garlic clove

EQUIPMENT NEEDED: A medium saucepan; a sterilized 1-quart jar with a lid; a coffee filter; a sieve; a bottle with a nonmetallic lid

Bring the vinegar to just below the boiling point in a medium saucepan. Loosely pack the leaves and stems of the salad burnet, basil, tarragon and thyme in a sterilized 1-quart jar. Bruise the herbs lightly. Add the chile and garlic. Fill the jar with the vinegar and seal with the lid. Let stand for 2 to 3 weeks to infuse. Strain the vinegar through a coffee filter in a sieve into a bowl, discarding the solids. Pour into a bottle with a nonmetallic lid and store at room temperature.

Note: Our all-time favorite vinegar, it can be used in any recipe that calls for red wine vinegar.

Pineapple Salsa

MAKES 2 CUPS

1 cup finely chopped fresh pineapple
1/4 cup chopped red bell pepper
1 tablespoon minced red onion
1 small jalapeño chile, seeded and
    finely chopped

1 tablespoon lemon juice or lime juice
1 teaspoon honey
2 tablespoons finely chopped fresh cilantro or
    fresh mint leaves

Combine the pineapple, bell pepper, onion, jalapeño chile, lemon juice and honey in a small bowl and mix well. Chill, covered, for 30 minutes for the flavors to meld. Stir in the cilantro just before serving.

Bourbon Pecans with Angostura Bitters

MAKES 4 1/2 CUPS

1/2 cup quality bourbon whiskey
1 pound pecan halves
1 tablespoon corn oil
1/2 tablespoon Worcestershire sauce
1/2 teaspoon angostura bitters
1/2 cup sugar

1/2 teaspoon ground cumin
1/2 teaspoon cayenne pepper, or a few drops of
    Tabasco sauce
1/2 teaspoon salt
Freshly ground black pepper to taste

EQUIPMENT NEEDED: A small saucepan; a large saucepan; a 10×15-inch baking pan

Simmer 1/2 cup bourbon in a small saucepan over medium heat for a few minutes or until reduced by one-fourth, watching carefully. (Meanwhile, pour 1 1/2 ounces bourbon into a 4-ounce glass and fill with water. Sip slowly while cooking.)

Blanch the pecans in boiling water in a large saucepan for 1 minute. Drain the pecans thoroughly. Combine the reduced bourbon, corn oil, Worcestershire sauce, bitters and sugar in a medium bowl. Add the pecans and toss to coat. Let stand for 10 minutes.

Preheat the oven to 325 degrees. Spread the coated pecans in a single layer in a 10×15-inch baking pan. Bake for 30 to 40 minutes or until the pecans are crisp and the liquid is absorbed, stirring every 10 minutes. Place the pecans in a large bowl. Mix the cumin, cayenne pepper, salt and black pepper in a small bowl. Sprinkle over the pecans and toss to coat.

Bitters
Bitters are a distillation of aromatic herbs, barks, roots, and other plants. They are prized for their unique bitter flavor and their ability to stimulate the appetite and aid digestion. Angostura bitters include gentian, a bitter herb that grows in Alpine regions.

Sweet basil (*Ocimum basilicum*)

Lemon Verbena Champagne Cocktail

SERVES 10 TO 12

1 cup sugar
2 cups water

20 to 25 organically grown fresh lemon
    verbena leaves
1 (750-milliliter) bottle Champagne, chilled

EQUIPMENT NEEDED: A small saucepan; a sieve; a pitcher; Champagne glasses

Bring the sugar and water to a boil in a small saucepan, stirring until the sugar dissolves. Remove from the heat. Add the lemon verbena leaves. Let stand, covered, until cool. Strain through a sieve into a pitcher, discarding the leaves. Store in the refrigerator. To serve, fill chilled Champagne glasses one-half full with the cold syrup and top with the Champagne.

Note: The essence of fresh lemon verbena will hit your nose just before your first sip of this cooling summer cocktail. You may want it all for yourself!

Mai-Bowle

SERVES 10 TO 12

12 sprigs of fresh sweet woodruff
1 pint (2 cups) Cognac
1 (750-milliliter) bottle of Champagne or
    sparkling water, chilled

2 (750-milliliter) bottles of Rhine or
    Moselle wine, chilled
12 large ripe strawberries

EQUIPMENT NEEDED: A sieve; a punch bowl; punch cups

Soak the woodruff in the cognac in a bowl for 8 to 10 hours. Strain into a punch bowl, discarding the woodruff. Add the chilled wines, strawberries and ice. Ladle into punch cups.

St. Louis Herb Society Tea-Pourri

MAKES 4 CUPS

1 whole cardamom pod
1 small cinnamon stick
3 whole cloves
8 to 10 fresh lemon verbena leaves, or
    6 dried lemon verbena leaves

2 teaspoons orange zest
4 teaspoons orange pekoe tea
2 teaspoons jasmine tea

EQUIPMENT NEEDED: A mortar with a pestle

Crush the cardamom, cinnamon stick, cloves, lemon verbena leaves and orange zest lightly in a mortar with a pestle. Add the orange pekoe tea and jasmine tea and crush lightly to mix. To use, make tea as usual, steeping for 3 to 5 minutes.

Note: To make dried orange or lemon zest, strip the outer peel of an orange or lemon with a carrot peeler. Place the strips on a baking sheet and let stand until dry and crisp in a warm place or bake in a 150- to 180-degree oven with the door ajar. When dry, pulverize in a mortar with a pestle or in a blender. Store in an airtight container out of light.

Basil and Strawberry Gimlet

SERVES 1

6 basil leaves
2 strawberries, hulled
Juice of 1 lime

2 ounces vodka or gin
2 tablespoons Simple Syrup (see sidebar)

EQUIPMENT NEEDED: A cocktail shaker, a muddler or wooden spoon; a martini glass

Place the basil in the bottom of a cocktail shaker. Add the strawberries and lime juice. Muddle by mashing with a muddler or wooden spoon. Add ice cubes, the vodka and simple syrup. Cover and shake several times or until the shaker feels icy cold. Strain into a chilled martini glass.

Note: Basil and lime make a perfect combination, and a touch of strawberry pulp turns this drink a lovely shade of pink.

Citrus Mint Vodka Martini

SERVES 1

8 citrus mint leaves, such as lemon,
   lime or orange
1 lime wedge

2 ounces vodka
1 tablespoon Simple Syrup (see sidebar)

EQUIPMENT NEEDED: A cocktail shaker; a muddler or wooden spoon; a martini glass

Place the mint leaves in the bottom of a cocktail shaker. Squeeze the lime wedge into the shaker and add the squeezed lime wedge. Muddle by mashing with a muddler or wooden spoon. Add ice cubes, the vodka and simple syrup. Cover and shake several times or until the shaker feels icy cold. Strain into a chilled martini glass.

Note: The mint julep meets the martini for this delightfully pale green cocktail with little flecks of mint.

 ## Simple Syrup
Bring two parts sugar and one part water to a boil in a small saucepan, stirring until the sugar dissolves. Remove from the heat to cool. Store in the refrigerator.

Peach Liqueur with Herbs

1/2 cup sugar
1/2 cup honey
1 cup water
5 fresh bay leaves
3 stevia leaves

1/2 teaspoon ground mace
6 large peaches, peeled and sliced
3 peppercorns, or a dash of brandy
Vodka

EQUIPMENT NEEDED: A small saucepan; a 1-quart wide-mouth canning jar with a lid; a sieve; a small pitcher

Bring the sugar, honey and water to a boil in a small saucepan to form a thin syrup. Add the bay leaves, stevia and mace. Let stand, covered, until cool. Add the peaches. Macerate at room temperature for 8 to 12 hours. Remove the peaches and bay leaves to a wide-mouth canning jar using a slotted spoon. Pour 1/2 cup of the syrup over the peaches and bay leaves, discarding any unused syrup. Add the peppercorns. Fill the jar with vodka. Seal the jar and let stand to mellow for at least 1 week before using. Strain through a sieve into a small pitcher, discarding the solids. Chill in the refrigerator. Serve over crushed ice.

Note: When infusing herbs, always cover the pan so essential oils will not escape.

Sweet Mary

1 cup tomato juice
1/2 teaspoon Tabasco sauce
4 cups tomato juice
1 cup bottled clam juice
Juice of 1 lime
2 tablespoons apple juice
2 tablespoons fresh salad burnet leaves

1 teaspoon fresh cilantro leaves
1 teaspoon grated fresh gingerroot
1/2 teaspoon salt
1/4 teaspoon Tabasco sauce
4 lovage straws for garnish (see Note)
4 twists of lime for garnish

EQUIPMENT NEEDED: An ice cube tray; a 6-cup food processor; a sieve; four tall (10-ounce) glasses

Mix 1 cup tomato juice and 1/2 teaspoon Tabasco sauce in a small bowl. Pour into an ice cube tray. Freeze for 8 hours or until firm.

Process 4 cups tomato juice, the clam juice, lime juice, apple juice, salad burnet leaves, cilantro leaves, gingerroot, salt and 1/4 teaspoon Tabasco sauce in a 6-cup food processor for 3 minutes or until smooth. Place the tomato ice cubes in four tall (10-ounce) glasses. Strain the juice mixture through a sieve into the glasses. Garnish each with a lovage straw and a twist of lime.

Note: A lovely alternative to the traditional Bloody Mary, we like to make tomato ice cubes so the drink stays thick and is not diluted with water. Spike with vodka to taste, if desired. To make lovage straws, cut long sections of hollow lovage stalks from a mature plant. They add hints of cucumber and celery flavors.

Soups & Breads

Rosemary and Ginger Tilapia Soup, page 42

Rosemary and Ginger Tilapia Soup

1 tablespoon butter
2 small zucchini, cut into quarters lengthwise and thinly sliced
6 scallions, thinly sliced
6 radishes, cut into halves and thinly sliced
1 tablespoon minced fresh gingerroot
1 tablespoon chopped fresh rosemary
1 tablespoon chopped fresh thyme
4 cups fish stock (preferably homemade)
Juice of 1 lemon
Juice of 1 lime
1 or 2 dashes of soy sauce
Salt and freshly ground pepper to taste
2 tilapia fillets (about 8 ounces), cut into halves lengthwise
    and sliced across into bite-size pieces
4 to 6 thin lemon slices for garnish
4 to 6 thin lime slices for garnish
4 to 6 thin radish slices for garnish

EQUIPMENT NEEDED: A medium saucepan

Melt the butter in a medium saucepan over medium-high heat. Add the zucchini, scallions, radishes, gingerroot, rosemary and thyme. Cook just until tender, stirring frequently. Add the stock, lemon juice, lime juice and soy sauce. Bring to a simmer. Sprinkle with salt and pepper.

Just before serving, add the fish and remove from the heat. Let stand for 2 to 3 minutes or until the fish cooks through. Ladle immediately into serving bowls. Garnish each with a slice each of lemon, lime and radish.

Note: This soup can be made all year long if you use seasonal fish or seafood. Try shrimp, scallops, mussels, halibut, trout, or salmon.

Lemon Grass Shrimp Soup

2 shallots, sliced
1 tablespoon sesame oil
1 stalk lemon grass, cut into diagonal slivers
2 garlic cloves, minced
1 tablespoon minced fresh gingerroot
1 kaffir lime leaf, finely shredded
2 cups shrimp stock or chicken stock
　 (preferably homemade)

2 cups coconut milk
Juice of 1 lime
8 ounces uncooked shrimp, peeled
　 and deveined
1 (8-ounce) can straw mushrooms, drained, or
　 $1/2$ cup button mushrooms, thinly sliced
Sea salt and freshly ground pepper to taste
$1/4$ cup chopped fresh cilantro for garnish

EQUIPMENT NEEDED: A large saucepan

Sauté the shallots in the sesame oil in a large saucepan over medium-high heat until translucent. Add the lemon grass, garlic, gingerroot and kaffir lime leaf. Heat slightly to release the fragrances. Add the stock, coconut milk and lime juice. Bring to a simmer. Do not boil. (The soup may be made in advance up to this point.) Add the shrimp and mushrooms. Simmer for 4 minutes or until the shrimp turn pink. (The shrimp cook quickly and should be added just before serving.) Sprinkle with sea salt and pepper. Ladle into serving bowls. Garnish with the cilantro.

Note: When paired with lemon grass, the kaffir lime leaf gives this soup its refreshing character. One tablespoon of lime zest may be substituted, but you will miss the fantastic burst of flavor.

 ## Lemon Grass

Fresh lemon grass can be found in many international markets. Use the white part of the stalk up to the first split to flavor teas, sauces, and curries. Use very thin slivers of the green part in soups. To grow your own, begin in early spring. Prepare a sixteen- to twenty-inch clay pot with sandy soil. Poke stalks about three inches into the soil and then water. Place in a sunny location and keep watered.

Chicken Kale Soup with Cannellini Beans

SERVES 6 TO 8

1 tablespoon olive oil
1 whole chicken breast
1 teaspoon dried oregano
Salt and freshly ground pepper to taste
8 ounces spicy salami such as Sopressato or
 Calabrese, chopped into 1/2-inch pieces
2 tablespoons olive oil
1 yellow onion, chopped
2 carrots, peeled and chopped
2 ribs celery, chopped

5 garlic cloves, minced
2 teaspoons fresh thyme, coarsely chopped
Leaves of 1 sprig of rosemary, chopped
3 fresh sage leaves, chopped
1 (15-ounce) can cannellini beans, rinsed
 and drained
6 cups chicken stock or broth
 (preferably homemade)
12 ounces kale, veins removed and
 leaves chopped

EQUIPMENT NEEDED: A small baking pan; a medium skillet; a large saucepan

Preheat the oven to 400 degrees. Drizzle 1 tablespoon olive oil over the chicken and rub in with your fingers. Sprinkle with the oregano, salt and pepper. Place in a small baking pan. Bake for 15 minutes or until the chicken is cooked through. Remove the chicken and let stand until cool, reserving the baking drippings. Cut the chicken into bite-size pieces, discarding the skin and bones.

Fry the salami in 2 tablespoons olive oil in a medium skillet over medium-high heat for 2 minutes or until crisp. Remove to paper towels to drain, reserving the drippings in the skillet.

Cook the onion, carrots and celery in the reserved salami drippings in the skillet for 5 minutes or until softened. Add the garlic, thyme, rosemary and sage. Cook for 1 to 2 minutes, stirring constantly. Spoon into a large saucepan. Add the beans, stock and reserved baking drippings. Bring to a boil; reduce the heat. Simmer for 5 minutes. Add the kale. Simmer until the kale wilts. Stir in the chicken, salami, salt and pepper. Ladle into serving bowls.

Note: This is a hearty and filling soup with lots of flavor.

 ## Kale
An essential element in southern cooking, kale, as well as other spring greens, is fast becoming popular in many dishes throughout the country. It is a member of the cabbage family, yet its leaves do not form a head. Most greens can be substituted in recipes, but each has its own distinctive flavor, so we suggest that you experiment. Greens still attached to their roots and placed in the refrigerator keep best. Never wash greens until you are ready to use them.

Butternut Squash and Black Bean Chili

SERVES 10

3 tablespoons extra-virgin olive oil
1 yellow onion, chopped
2 garlic cloves, minced
1 jalapeño chile, seeded and minced
1 chipotle chile, chopped
8 cups (1/2-inch) fresh butternut squash cubes
6 plum tomatoes, chopped and juices reserved
3 tablespoons tomato paste
1 cup chicken broth (preferably homemade)
1/4 cup ancho chili powder

2 tablespoons ground cumin
2 tablespoons coarse salt
2 tablespoons apple cider vinegar
2 teaspoons dried epazote
1 ounce bittersweet chocolate
4 (15-ounce) cans black beans, rinsed
  and drained
10 ounces crumbled goat cheese, or 1/2 cup
  sour cream for garnish
Jalapeño and Cheddar Corn Bread (page 55)

EQUIPMENT NEEDED: A large stockpot

Heat the olive oil in a large stockpot over medium heat. Add the onion, garlic, jalapeño chile and chipotle chile. Sauté for 10 minutes or until the vegetables are softened. Add the butternut squash, undrained tomatoes, tomato paste, broth, chili powder, cumin, salt, vinegar and epazote. Bring to a low boil. Reduce the heat and simmer, covered, for 20 minutes or until the squash is tender. Add the chocolate and black beans. Cook until the chocolate melts, stirring constantly and adding water if needed for the desired consistency. Simmer, covered, for 30 minutes. Ladle into serving bowls. Garnish each serving with the goat cheese. Serve with Jalapeño and Cheddar Corn Bread.

Note: Native to Central America, epazote is an easily grown, shrubby, annual plant whose name means "smelly animal" in Aztec. Pungent and slightly bitter with hints of lemon, its popularity in Mexican culture is due to its ability to lessen the digestive effects of beans.

Curried Cauliflower Soup with Honeycrisp Apples

2 tablespoons unsalted butter
2 tablespoons olive oil
2 yellow onions, chopped
3 Honeycrisp apples or other crisp sweet
    apples, such as Pink Lady
Florets of 1 large head cauliflower,
    coarsely chopped

1 tablespoon St. Louis Herb Society Curry
    Powder (page 49) or store-bought equivalent
1 fresh bay leaf
4 cups chicken stock (preferably homemade)
1 cup heavy cream
Salt and freshly ground pepper to taste
Fresh lemon juice for coating

EQUIPMENT NEEDED: A large saucepan; an immersion blender, food processor or electric blender

Melt the butter with the olive oil in a large saucepan. Add the onions and cook until soft. Peel, core and chop two of the apples. Stir the chopped apples, cauliflower and curry powder into the onions. Add the bay leaf and stock. Bring to a boil. Reduce the heat and simmer for 20 to 30 minutes or until the cauliflower is fork tender. Remove from the heat; discard the bay leaf. Purée the soup with an immersion blender or in a food processor or electric blender and return to the saucepan. Add the cream and heat through. Sprinkle with salt and pepper. Core and finely chop the remaining apple and place in a small bowl. Coat with lemon juice to prevent browning. Ladle the soup into serving bowls and garnish with the finely chopped apple.

Note: A surprising and versatile soup that can be served warm or chilled.

Corn Chowder with White Wine and Herbs

1/4 cup (1/2 stick) butter
1 1/2 cups minced yellow onions
1/3 cup all-purpose flour
3 cups chicken stock (preferably homemade)
1/2 cup dry white wine
1 green bell pepper, chopped
2 1/2 cups fresh or frozen corn kernels
    (from about 4 ears)

3 fresh sage leaves, chopped
1 tablespoon chopped fresh marjoram
3 tablespoons chopped fresh flat-leaf parsley
2 cups half-and-half
6 ounces Cheddar cheese, shredded
Salt and white pepper to taste
Saffron threads, fresh dill or shredded Cheddar
    cheese for garnish

EQUIPMENT NEEDED: A large saucepan; an immersion blender, food processor or electric blender

Melt the butter in a large saucepan over medium heat. Add the onions. Sauté for 5 minutes or until the onions are transparent. Add the flour. Cook for 3 minutes, stirring constantly. Whisk in the stock and wine gradually. Cook until slightly thickened, whisking constantly. Add the bell pepper, corn, sage, marjoram and parsley. Simmer for 15 minutes. Purée the soup with an immersion blender or in a food processor or electric blender and return to the saucepan. Stir in the half-and-half. Return the soup to a simmer. Remove from the heat. Stir in 6 ounces cheese until melted. Sprinkle with salt and white pepper. Ladle into serving bowls and garnish with saffron threads, fresh dill or shredded cheese.

Note: Our corn chowder has a delightfully herby fragrance intensified by the white wine. For a chunkier soup, forego using a blender.

Exotic Mushroom and Sage Soup

4 ounces shiitake mushrooms,
    coarsely chopped
4 ounces portobello mushrooms,
    coarsely chopped
1 yellow onion, chopped
1 carrot, chopped
2 ribs celery, chopped
8 cups chicken stock (preferably homemade)
8 fresh sage leaves

3 tablespoons unsalted butter
4 ounces cremini, stems removed and
    mushrooms chopped
5 tablespoons unsalted butter
1 cup all-purpose flour
3 cups milk
1/4 teaspoon Tabasco sauce
Salt and white pepper to taste

EQUIPMENT NEEDED: A 4-quart stockpot

Combine the shiitake mushrooms, portobello mushrooms, onion, carrot, celery and stock in a 4-quart stockpot. Bring to a boil. Reduce the heat and simmer, covered, for 15 minutes. Add the sage. Simmer for 15 minutes. Strain into a bowl, discarding the solids. Set the mushroom stock aside.

Melt 3 tablespoons butter in the stockpot over medium heat. Add the cremini mushrooms and sauté for 4 minutes. Remove the cremini mushrooms and set aside.

Melt 5 tablespoons butter in the stockpot over medium heat. Whisk in the flour to form a blonde roux. Cook for 3 to 5 minutes or until the mixture turns a caramel color. Whisk in the milk gradually. Cook until thickened and smooth, whisking constantly. Add the reserved mushroom stock gradually. Cook until thickened, stirring constantly. Add the reserved cremini mushrooms, Tabasco sauce, salt and white pepper. Cook until heated through. Ladle into serving bowls.

Note: Portobello mushrooms are a larger, more mature cremini. Do not clean mushrooms with water, and never soak them, or they will absorb water and become mushy. Instead, use a pastry brush to remove any dirt.

Herbal Oil Pastes
Herbal oil pastes are thick mixtures of fresh herbs and oil. Use olive oil or canola oil for basil, cilantro, oregano, or parsley. Use olive oil for mint, sorrel, lemon balm, and lemon verbena. Process the herbs in a food processor until chopped and add enough oil to make a thick paste. Freeze in small sealable plastic freezer bags or jars and use when preparing soups or stews.

Creamy Roasted Tomato Soup with Fennel Crostini

SOUP
3 pounds large firm ripe tomatoes, cut into halves and seeded
Olive oil for brushing
1/4 cup (1/2 stick) unsalted butter
White parts of 3 leeks, rinsed thoroughly and chopped
2 parsnips, peeled and chopped
1 fennel bulb, chopped (feathery tops reserved for crostini)
3 cups chicken stock (preferably homemade)

3 sprigs of fennel tops
8 sprigs of fresh flat-leaf parsley
Salt and freshly ground pepper to taste
1 1/2 cups heavy whipping cream

FENNEL CROSTINI
18 (1/4-inch) slices French baguette
Olive oil for brushing
5 garlic cloves, cut into halves
1/2 cup (2 ounces) grated asiago cheese
Feathery tops of fennel, chopped

EQUIPMENT NEEDED: A large shallow baking pan; a large saucepan; an immersion blender or electric blender; a large baking sheet

To prepare the soup, preheat the oven to 425 degrees. Place the tomatoes in a single layer cut side down in a large shallow baking pan. Brush with olive oil. Bake for 30 minutes or until the skins begin to darken, turning several times. Remove from the oven to cool. Remove and discard the skins, reserving the tomato pulp and juices.

Melt the butter in a large saucepan over medium heat. Add the leeks, parsnips and fennel bulb. Sauté until very soft. Add the stock, fennel tops and parsley. Bring to a boil. Reduce the heat and simmer for 30 minutes. Remove and discard the herb sprigs. Add the reserved tomatoes and juices. Purée with an immersion blender or in an electric blender and return to the saucepan. Sprinkle with salt and pepper. Stir in the cream and keep warm.

To prepare the crostini, preheat the oven to 400 degrees. Brush the top and bottom of each baguette slice with olive oil and arrange on a large baking sheet. Rub each with the cut side of the garlic cloves. Sprinkle with the cheese and fennel tops. Bake for 5 minutes or until brown.

To serve, ladle the soup into serving bowls and float two or three crostini on top of each serving.

Note: Make this soup when you have a bumper crop of the finest homegrown tomatoes. Roasting the tomatoes brings out their sweetness in a unique way.

 Fennel
In the garden, fennel looks very similar to dill, but its leaves are thinner and its taste is quite different. All parts of fennel—seeds, leaves, and bulb—are aromatic and edible. A main ingredient in absinthe, fennel's anise-like flavor made it ideal in ancient times to make unsavory food more appealing. Today we admire it for its unique ability to add dimension to salads, soups, and stews. Never grow fennel near dill, as neither will thrive. The same fate will befall fennel and coriander.

Creamed Curry Wild Rice Soup

4 cups water
1 teaspoon salt
1 cup wild rice
6 tablespoons unsalted butter
1 onion, chopped
1/2 cup sliced celery
2 cups sliced assorted exotic mushrooms
1/4 cup all-purpose flour
51/2 cups chicken broth (preferably homemade)

1 teaspoon St. Louis Herb Society
   Curry Powder (recipe follows) or
   store-bought equivalent
1/2 teaspoon dry mustard
1/2 teaspoon white pepper
Salt to taste
2 cups heavy cream or half-and-half
   (do not use milk)
1 cup dry sherry

EQUIPMENT NEEDED: A medium saucepan; a heavy medium stockpot

Bring the water and 1 teaspoon salt to a boil in a medium saucepan. Add the rice and reduce the heat. Simmer, covered, for 30 minutes. Drain any excess water and set aside.

Melt the butter in a heavy medium stockpot over medium heat. Add the onion and celery and sauté until golden brown. Add the mushrooms and sauté for 5 minutes. Stir in the flour. Cook for several minutes or until the flour is absorbed, stirring constantly. Add the broth gradually, stirring constantly. Stir in the cooked rice, curry powder, dry mustard, white pepper and salt to taste. Return to a simmer; reduce the heat. Stir in the cream and sherry and cook until heated through. Ladle into soup bowls.

Note: This soup is best stored in the refrigerator for 8 to 10 hours, where it mysteriously thickens. If it is too thick after reheating, simply add more cream and sherry.

St. Louis Herb Society Curry Powder

4 ounces ground coriander
4 ounces ground cumin
4 ounces turmeric
2 ounces ginger
1 ounce black pepper
1 ounce ground fennel seed

1/2 ounce cayenne pepper
1/2 ounce ground cloves
1/2 ounce fenugreek
1/2 ounce mace
1/2 ounce dry mustard
1/2 ounce poppy seeds

EQUIPMENT NEEDED: Airtight containers

Mix the coriander, cumin, turmeric, ginger, black pepper, fennel, cayenne pepper, cloves, fenugreek, mace, dry mustard and poppy seeds together in a bowl. Store in airtight containers.

Arugula and Roasted Banana Soup

2 ripe (but not brown) bananas
2 tablespoons butter
1 yellow onion, chopped
2 or 3 garlic cloves, minced
4 cups chicken stock (preferably homemade)
2 cups arugula, washed thoroughly to remove grit and
    coarsely chopped
Salt and freshly ground pepper to taste
Crushed dried bananas for garnish
Arugula for garnish

EQUIPMENT NEEDED: A small baking pan; a large saucepan; an immersion blender, food processor or electric blender

Preheat the oven to 400 degrees. Peel the bananas and place in a small baking pan. Roast for 10 to 20 minutes or until caramelized. Melt the butter in a large saucepan over medium heat. Add the onion and garlic and cook until soft. Stir in the undrained roasted bananas. Add the stock and return to a simmer. Add 2 cups arugula. Cook until wilted, stirring constantly. Purée the soup with an immersion blender or in a food processor or electric blender and return to the saucepan. Sprinkle with salt and pepper. Ladle into soup bowls. Garnish with dried bananas and additional arugula.

Note: The peppery zip of arugula and the sweetness of roasted bananas make an unusual but delicious combination for this soup.

Chilled Avocado Soup
with Lemon Verbena and Sorrel

3 cups water
1 tablespoon sea salt
1 sweet yellow onion, finely chopped
6 ribs celery, finely chopped
2 carrots, peeled and grated
4 garlic cloves, minced
1 cup loosely packed fresh sorrel leaves
1 cup loosely packed fresh lemon
   verbena leaves

1 fresh bay leaf
3/4 cup finely ground toasted almonds (about
   1 1/2 cups whole almonds)
4 large ripe avocados, chopped
Half-and-half
Juice of 2 large lemons, or to taste
Sea salt to taste
Chopped flat-leaf parsley or chives for garnish

EQUIPMENT NEEDED: A large saucepan; an immersion blender, food processor or electric blender

Bring the water and 1 tablespoon sea salt to a boil in a large saucepan. Add the onion, celery, carrots, garlic, sorrel leaves, verbena leaves and bay leaf and return to a boil. Reduce the heat. Simmer for 30 minutes or until the vegetables are very tender. Remove and discard the lemon verbena leaves and bay leaf. Add the almonds. Purée with an immersion blender until smooth. Chill for 2 hours or until chilled through.

To serve, add the avocadoes to the chilled soup base. Purée with an immersion blender or in a food processor or electric blender and return to the saucepan. Stir in a few tablespoons of half-and-half if the soup is too thick. Add the lemon juice and sea salt to taste. Ladle into serving bowls and garnish with parsley.

Note: The texture of this soup should be like that of hot chocolate—creamy but not too thick. It will keep in the refrigerator for two days.

Avocado
The avocado was originally called the "alligator pear." For centuries it was known only by this name. When marketing the fruit became an issue for growers in the 1800s, the name was changed to a more appealing one. The avocado became a popular crop in Southern California, something that might not have happened were it still called an "alligator pear." High in fat, its creamy texture makes it ideal for spreads, soups, and vegetarian dishes.

Meyer Lemon and Blueberry Soup

6 cups blueberries
5 cups water
1 cup sugar
2 Meyer lemons, rinsed and thinly sliced
2 tablespoons chopped fresh lemon verbena leaves
1 (3-inch) stick cinnamon
1/2 teaspoon freshly grated nutmeg
4 1/2 cups sour cream
1 cup dry red wine, such as Pinot Noir

EQUIPMENT NEEDED: A large saucepan; a sieve

Combine the blueberries, water, sugar, lemons, lemon verbena, cinnamon and nutmeg in a large saucepan. Bring to a boil over high heat. Reduce the heat to medium and simmer for 15 minutes. Strain through a sieve into a large bowl, discarding the solids. Chill, covered, for 1 hour or longer. Whisk in the sour cream and wine until smooth. Chill, covered, until ready to serve. Ladle into serving bowls.

Note: Meyer lemons are rounder, smoother, and sweeter than regular lemons. If Meyers are not in season, use regular lemons and increase the amount of sugar.

 ## Herbs in Chilled Foods
Chilled foods will need approximately twice the amount of herbs as hot or warm foods. If a recipe calls for dried herbs and you can use fresh, double or triple the amount according to personal preference and the potency of the herbs. Adding fresh herbs toward the end of cooking provides the strongest and best flavor.

Meyer lemon (*Citrus × meyeri*)

Cranberry Basil Gazpacho

1 small yellow onion, minced
1 small green bell pepper, chopped
1 cucumber, seeded and chopped
4 tomatoes, peeled, seeded and chopped
2 cups cranberry juice cocktail

1/4 cup olive oil
Juice of 1 lemon
2 tablespoons fresh basil, chiffonade cut
1 tablespoon coarsely chopped fresh dill

Combine the onion, bell pepper, cucumber, tomatoes, cranberry juice cocktail, olive oil, lemon juice, basil and dill in a large nonreactive bowl and mix well. Chill, covered, in the refrigerator. Serve cold.

Note: Easy and delicious, our gazpacho has a twist of cranberry.

Cool and Creamy Watermelon Soup

1 seedless watermelon
1 large jalapeño chile, seeded and
   coarsely chopped
1 garlic clove

1 tablespoon coarsely chopped cilantro leaves,
  or to taste
3/4 to 1 cup sour cream
Salt to taste

EQUIPMENT NEEDED: A food processor or electric blender

Cut the watermelon flesh into large chunks and set aside. Reserve a few slices of the rind with white and pink portions for garnish.

Pulse the jalapeño chile, garlic and cilantro in a food processor or blender several times until blended. Add about 3/4 cup of the watermelon chunks and process until blended. Add 3/4 cup sour cream and salt and process until blended. Add more cilantro and sour cream, if desired. Pour the soup into a medium bowl. Cut the remaining watermelon chunks into small pieces and add to the soup. Chill or freeze until serving time. Cut the reserved watermelon rind into small, thin strips. Chill until ready to serve.

To serve, pour the soup into chilled tumblers or margarita glasses. Garnish with the watermelon rind strips.

Note: Jalapeño chiles and cilantro give this pink soup a touch of green and a little kick!

Jalapeño and Cheddar Corn Bread

1¹/4 cups stone-ground cornmeal
Kernels from 2 ears of fresh corn
3/4 cup all-purpose flour
2 teaspoons baking powder
¹/2 teaspoon baking soda
3/4 teaspoon coarse salt
1 teaspoon chopped fresh flat-leaf parsley
¹/2 teaspoon chopped fresh thyme
2 eggs, lightly beaten
1 cup buttermilk
¹/2 cup (2 ounces) shredded medium-sharp Cheddar cheese
1 tablespoon minced jalapeño chiles from a jar
2 tablespoons butter, melted
1 tablespoon honey
1 tablespoon canola oil

EQUIPMENT NEEDED: A 9-inch cast-iron skillet; a wire rack

Grease a 9-inch cast-iron skillet with shortening or nonstick cooking spray and place in a cold oven. Heat the oven to 425 degrees.

Whisk the cornmeal, corn, flour, baking powder, baking soda, salt, parsley and thyme in a large bowl. Make a well in the center and set aside. Combine the eggs, buttermilk, cheese, jalapeño chiles, butter, honey and canola oil in a small bowl and mix well. Pour into the well of dry ingredients and stir until just combined. Do not overmix. Pour into the hot skillet and return to the oven. Reduce the oven temperature to 400 degrees. Bake for 35 minutes or until a wooden pick inserted in the center comes out clean. Remove from the oven and place on a wire rack. Let stand for 5 minutes to cool. Loosen the edge from the side of the skillet and invert onto the wire rack. Cut into ten wedges and serve with softened butter.

Note: Fresh corn kernels and jalapeño chiles from a jar make this corn bread delightfully moist.

Basil Popovers with Garlic Chive Butter

GARLIC CHIVE BUTTER
1/2 cup (1 stick) unsalted butter, softened
2 tablespoons finely chopped garlic chives
Pinch of salt

POPOVERS
1 1/4 cups all-purpose flour
1/2 teaspoon salt

3 eggs
1 1/4 cups milk
1 tablespoon unsalted butter, melted
1/4 cup chopped fresh basil leaves
1/4 cup chopped fresh garlic chives
  (stems only)
2 tablespoons unsalted butter

EQUIPMENT NEEDED: An electric hand mixer; a 6-cup popover pan; butter-flavor nonstick cooking spray

To prepare the garlic chive butter, combine the butter, garlic chives and salt in a small bowl and mix well. Chill, covered, until serving time. Make ahead so the flavors can meld.

To prepare the popovers, mix the flour and salt in a medium mixing bowl. Beat the eggs with the milk in a mixing bowl with an electric hand mixer until light and frothy. Add 1 tablespoon melted butter and beat at low speed until well mixed. Add to the flour mixture and beat at medium speed for 1 to 2 minutes or until the batter is the consistency of heavy cream. Add the basil and garlic chives and mix gently by hand. (The batter may be made in advance up to this point and chilled in the refrigerator. Bring to room temperature before baking.)

Place an oven rack in the middle of the oven. Preheat the oven to 400 degrees. Spray the popover cups with butter-flavor nonstick cooking spray. Heat the popover pan in the oven for 2 minutes. Cut 2 tablespoons butter into six equal pieces. Place one butter piece in each preheated popover cup. Return the pan to the oven and heat for 1 minute or until the butter is bubbly. Fill each cup one-half full with the batter. Bake for 20 minutes. Do not open the oven door. Reduce the oven temperature to 300 degrees. Bake for 20 minutes longer. Serve immediately with the garlic chive butter.

Note: There are three rules to making good popovers: ingredients should be at room temperature; fill cups no more than one-half full; and do not open the oven door. When garlic chives are in season, their blossoms make a lovely garnish. The popovers are best served immediately, but can be held in the oven for up to 30 minutes. Turn off the oven. Pierce the side of each popover to allow the steam to escape and set back in the pan. Let the oven cool for 5 minutes and return the pan to the oven.

Variation for the garlic chive butter: Instead of garlic chives, try 1 tablespoon finely chopped basil leaves with a few drops of garlic juice, or 1/8 teaspoon porcini mushroom powder with garlic chives and garlic juice.

Garlic chives (*Allium tuberosum*)

Sweet Cream Biscuits with Lemon Verbena MAKES 1 DOZEN

2 tablespoons finely chopped lemon
   verbena leaves
Zest of 1 lemon
1/4 cup sugar
2 cups all-purpose flour
1 teaspoon baking powder
1/2 teaspoon salt

1/2 cup (1 stick) unsalted butter, chilled and
   cut into cubes
1 egg, beaten
1/2 cup half-and-half
Melted butter for brushing
Sugar for sprinkling

EQUIPMENT NEEDED: A 2-inch biscuit cutter; a large baking sheet

Preheat the oven to 425 degrees. Mix the verbena leaves, lemon zest and sugar in a medium bowl. Add the flour, baking powder and salt and mix well. Cut in 1/2 cup butter until the mixture resembles small peas. Add the egg and half-and-half and stir just until combined. Knead on a lightly floured surface a few times to form a dough. Pat into a 1/2-inch-thick circle. Cut with a floured 2-inch biscuit cutter and place on a large baking sheet. Bake for 12 to 15 minutes or until light golden brown. Remove from the oven. Brush the hot biscuits with melted butter and sprinkle with sugar.

Note: You may serve these biscuits with butter, crème fraîche, or sour cream, but they are good enough all by themselves.

Chive Biscuits MAKES 2 DOZEN

2 cups sifted all-purpose flour
4 teaspoons baking powder
1 tablespoon sugar
1/2 teaspoon salt

1/2 cup shortening
1 egg, beaten
3/4 cup milk
1/4 cup chopped fresh chives

EQUIPMENT NEEDED: A large baking sheet

Preheat the oven to 450 degrees. Sift the flour, baking powder, sugar and salt together into a bowl. Cut in the shortening until the mixture resembles coarse crumbs. Combine the egg, milk and chives in a small bowl and mix well. Add to the flour mixture all at once and stir with a fork until the dough follows the fork around the bowl. Drop the dough by tablespoonfuls onto an ungreased baking sheet. Bake for 10 to 14 minutes or until golden brown.

Minted Berry Muffins

2 cups unbleached all-purpose flour
2 teaspoons baking powder
1/2 teaspoon salt
1/2 cup (1 stick) unsalted butter, softened
3/4 cup granulated sugar
1/2 cup packed brown sugar

2 eggs
1 teaspoon pure vanilla extract
1/2 cup milk
21/2 cups raspberries or blueberries
1/4 cup finely chopped mint leaves

EQUIPMENT NEEDED: An electric hand mixer; a 12-cup standard muffin pan; paper muffin liners; a wire rack

Preheat the oven to 375 degrees. Mix the flour, baking powder and salt together in a medium mixing bowl. Cream the butter in a large mixing bowl with an electric hand mixer. Add the granulated sugar and brown sugar and beat at high speed until light and fluffy. Add the eggs one at a time, beating well at high speed after each addition. Beat in the vanilla. Add 1/4 cup of the milk and one-half of the flour mixture. Stir with a wooden spoon just until combined. Add the remaining 1/4 cup milk and the remaining flour mixture and stir just until combined. Do not overmix or the muffins will be tough. Mash 2 cups of the berries in a bowl by hand. Stir into the batter. Fold in the remaining whole berries and the mint. Spoon into paper-lined muffin cups, filling two-thirds full. Bake for 25 to 35 minutes or until golden brown and a tester inserted in the centers come out clean. Cool in the muffin pan for 10 minutes. Remove to a wire rack to cool completely.

Note: In addition to spearmint and peppermint, there are several new and unusual varieties of mint. Try orange, lemon,...or even chocolate mint!

Herbal Citrus Scones

2 cups unbleached all-purpose flour
2 tablespoons sugar
2 teaspoons baking powder
1/2 teaspoon salt
1/4 cup (1/2 stick) butter, slightly softened
2 eggs, beaten
1/3 cup milk or light cream

2 tablespoons minced fresh herbs, such as
    lemon balm, basil, mint or sage
Grated zest of 1 orange
Grated zest of 1 lemon or lime
Egg wash for glaze
Sugar for sprinkling

EQUIPMENT NEEDED: A pastry blender; a large baking sheet

Preheat the oven to 425 degrees. Mix the flour, 2 tablespoons sugar, the baking powder and salt in a mixing bowl. Cut the butter into 1/2-inch cubes and distribute over the flour mixture. Cut in the butter with a pastry blender until the mixture resembles coarse crumbs. Stir in the eggs. Fold in the milk, herbs and citrus zest just until combined. Do not overmix.

Roll the dough into a circle 1/2 inch thick on a floured surface. Cut into six wedges with a sharp knife. Brush the wedges with egg wash and sprinkle with sugar. Place on a lightly greased large baking sheet. Bake for 10 to 12 minutes or until light brown.

Cherry Scones with Lemon Verbena Honey Butter

LEMON VERBENA HONEY BUTTER
1/2 cup (1 stick) unsalted butter, softened
2 tablespoons honey
Zest of 1 lemon
1 teaspoon finely chopped lemon
    verbena leaves
Pinch of salt

SCONES
2 cups all-purpose flour
1/4 cup sugar

2 teaspoons baking powder
1/8 teaspoon salt
1/3 cup unsalted butter, chilled and cut
    into cubes
1 cup coarsely chopped dried cherries
1/2 cup heavy cream
1 egg
1 1/2 teaspoons pure vanilla extract
Egg wash for glaze
1/3 cup sliced almonds
Sugar for sprinkling

EQUIPMENT NEEDED: A large baking sheet; baking parchment; a wire rack

To prepare the butter, blend the butter and honey in a small bowl. Add the lemon zest, lemon verbena and salt and mix well. Store, covered, in the refrigerator until serving time.

To prepare the scones, preheat the oven to 425 degrees. Mix the flour, 1/4 cup sugar, the baking powder and salt in a large bowl. Cut in the butter until the mixture resembles coarse crumbs. Stir in the dried cherries. Whisk the cream, egg and vanilla in a small bowl. Add to the flour mixture and stir to combine. Knead lightly on a floured surface a few times. Pat into a circle 1 inch thick. Cut into six to eight wedges using a sharp knife. Place the wedges on a baking sheet lined with baking parchment. Brush with egg wash. Sprinkle with the almonds and sugar. Bake for 13 to 15 minutes or until light brown. Remove from the pan to a wire rack to cool. Serve with the lemon verbena honey butter.

Note: Scones should be baked in a hot oven so the dough sets quickly and the scones are light. Do not overmix or the scones will be tough.

Lemon Cardamom Tea Bread

BREAD
1 1/3 cups honey
3/4 cup (1 1/2 sticks) unsalted butter, softened
2 eggs
1/2 cup milk
2 tablespoons fresh lemon juice
3 cups all-purpose flour
3/4 teaspoon baking soda
1/4 teaspoon salt
2 teaspoons ground cardamom

1 cup chopped toasted English walnuts
2 teaspoons chopped fresh lemon verbena
    leaves or lemon thyme
1/2 cup finely chopped candied lemon peel,
    or 1/4 cup fresh lemon zest
    (about 4 medium lemons)

LEMON GLAZE
Juice of 2 lemons
Confectioners' sugar

EQUIPMENT NEEDED: Two (4×8-inch) loaf pans

To prepare the bread, preheat the oven to 325 degrees. Combine the honey, butter, eggs, milk and lemon juice in a large bowl and mix well with a wooden spoon. Mix the flour, baking soda, salt and cardamom together in a bowl. Add to the honey mixture and mix by hand until light and creamy. Stir in the walnuts, lemon verbena and candied lemon peel. Divide the batter evenly between two greased and lightly floured 4×8-inch loaf pans. Tap the bottoms of the pans sharply against a hard surface to settle the batter. Bake for 1 hour or until testers inserted in the centers come out clean. Cool the loaves in the pans on a wire rack for 10 minutes.

To prepare the glaze, place the lemon juice in a small bowl. Stir in enough confectioners' sugar to form a thick but pourable glaze. Invert the loaves onto the wire rack and pour the glaze over the loaves. Let cool completely.

Note: You may omit the glaze and serve the bread with butter.

 ## Cardamom
Prized for its intensely fragrant aroma, cardamom is a staple in Indian cooking as well as Nordic baking. Be careful to use only Indian Elettaria cardamom, also known as green, or true, cardamom. Since cardamom is second only to saffron in cost, it is often adulterated. It is best to buy and store the whole pods. For the best flavor, toast the seeds until they are aromatic, and then grind them.

Focaccia with Brushed Herb Topping

MAKES 24 (2¹/2-INCH) SQUARES OR 1 LOAF

1 cup warm water (105 to 115 degrees)
1 teaspoon sugar
1 envelope dry yeast
3 to 4 cups bread flour
1 teaspoon salt
1 teaspoon olive oil
2 tablespoons (about) cornmeal

2 tablespoons olive oil
1 garlic clove, crushed
1 teaspoon chopped fresh basil leaves
1 teaspoon chopped fresh oregano
2 tablespoons coarse salt
¹/4 cup (1 ounce) freshly grated
    Parmesan cheese

EQUIPMENT NEEDED: A 10×15-inch baking pan or loaf pan

Mix the water and sugar in a small bowl. Sprinkle the yeast over the top and stir to dissolve. Let stand in a warm place to proof for 5 to 10 minutes or until the yeast swells and becomes bubbly.

Mix 1 cup of the flour and 1 teaspoon salt in a large bowl. Stir in the yeast mixture and 1 teaspoon olive oil. Add the remaining flour gradually until the dough becomes too stiff to stir, stirring well after each addition. Knead the dough on a well-floured surface for 10 minutes or until smooth and elastic, incorporating the flour as necessary. Place in a bowl greased with olive oil, turning to coat the surface. Cover with a dishtowel or plastic wrap. Let rise in a warm draft-free place for 1¹/2 hours or until doubled in bulk.

Roll the dough on a lightly floured surface into a 10×15-inch rectangle. Grease a 10×15-inch baking pan and sprinkle evenly with the cornmeal. Place the dough in the pan, stretching the dough evenly to cover the pan. Cover with a dishtowel or plastic wrap and let rest for 10 to 20 minutes. (For traditional bread, shape the dough into a loaf and place in a greased loaf pan. Let rise for 30 minutes or until doubled in bulk.)

Preheat the oven to 425 degrees. Combine 2 tablespoons olive oil, the garlic, basil and oregano in a small bowl and mix well. Uncover the dough and make indentations in the dough 1 inch apart using your index finger. Gently brush the herb mixture over the dough, making sure the herbs are evenly distributed. Sprinkle with the coarse salt and Parmesan cheese. Bake for 20 minutes or until light brown and crusty. (If using a loaf pan, bake for 30 minutes or until it sounds hollow when tapped.) Remove from the oven and cut into twenty-four squares using a sharp knife or pizza wheel. Best enjoyed while still warm.

Walnut Herb Bread

1 cup warm water (105 to 115 degrees)
Pinch of granulated sugar
1¹/2 envelopes dry yeast (1¹/2 tablespoons)
1 cup warm milk (105 to 115 degrees)
2 tablespoons brown sugar
1 tablespoon salt
3 tablespoons chopped fresh flat-leaf parsley

2 tablespoons chopped fresh basil leaves
1 tablespoon chopped fresh tarragon
1 garlic clove, minced
4¹/2 cups unbleached all-purpose flour
³/4 cup walnuts, lightly toasted and
  coarsely chopped

EQUIPMENT NEEDED: An electric stand mixer with paddle attachment (optional); a 1¹/2-quart baking dish or 9-inch springform pan; a wire rack

Mix the water and granulated sugar in a small bowl. Sprinkle the yeast over the top and stir to dissolve. Let stand in a warm place to proof for 5 to 10 minutes or until the yeast swells and becomes bubbly.

Combine the milk, brown sugar, salt, parsley, basil, tarragon, garlic and 1¹/2 cups of the flour in the bowl of an electric stand mixer and beat until smooth. Add the yeast mixture and the remaining 3 cups flour. Beat vigorously until the batter is smooth but still sticky. Cover the bowl with plastic wrap. Let rise in a warm place for 45 to 60 minutes or until doubled in bulk.

Sprinkle the walnuts over the top of the batter and beat vigorously to distribute evenly. Pour into a well-greased 1¹/2-quart baking dish or 9-inch springform pan. Let rise, loosely covered, in a warm place until the batter is even with the top of the pan.

Preheat the oven to 375 degrees. Bake the bread for 50 to 60 minutes or until the top is brown and crusty and a tester inserted in the center comes out clean. Invert the loaf out of the baking dish or release the side of the springform pan. Let cool on a wire rack.

Note: This savory bread is excellent with soft cheeses such as Gouda, provolone, or fontina. Serve warm to allow the cheese to soften into the bread.

 ## Basil Cigars
To preserve basil from a bumper crop, wash and dry the leaves and then roll them into a cylinder. Use unflavored dental floss to tie the bundle; freeze it in a sealable plastic bag. When fresh basil is needed for salads, soups, or pastas, cut off the dental floss and slice from the end of the "cigar."

Cheddar Herb Knotted Rolls

3^1/$_2$ to 4 cups all-purpose flour
1^1/$_2$ cups (6 ounces) shredded sharp Cheddar cheese
1 envelope dry yeast (1 tablespoon)
1^1/$_4$ cups milk
^{1}/$_4$ cup sugar
^{1}/$_2$ teaspoon salt
1 egg
1^1/$_2$ tablespoons dried herbs, such as dill, parsley,
    rosemary and thyme
Freshly grated Parmesan cheese for topping

EQUIPMENT NEEDED: An electric stand mixer with paddle attachment; a small saucepan; a large baking sheet

Combine 1 cup of the flour, the Cheddar cheese and yeast in the bowl of an electric stand mixer fitted with a paddle attachment and mix well by hand. Heat the milk, sugar and salt in a small saucepan to 105 to 115 degrees on a thermometer. Pour into the flour mixture. Beat at low speed for 30 seconds. Scrape down the side of the bowl. Add the egg and beat at high speed for 3 minutes. Beat in enough of the remaining flour to form a stiff dough. Knead in the herbs and additional flour as needed on a floured surface for 10 minutes or until the dough is smooth and elastic. Shape into a ball. Place in a greased bowl, turning to coat the surface. Cover with a damp towel. Let rise in a warm draft-free place for 40 minutes or until doubled in bulk.

Place the dough on a lightly floured surface and divide into two equal portions. Roll each portion into a cylinder. Cut each cylinder into twelve equal pieces. Roll each piece into a cylinder; tie into a knot. Place on a large baking sheet. Let rise for 20 to 25 minutes.

Preheat the oven to 375 degrees. Sprinkle the rolls with Parmesan cheese. Bake for 10 to 12 minutes or until golden brown.

Note: These rolls freeze well. Simply thaw and reheat.

Cinnamon Rolls

CINNAMON ROLLS
1/2 cup warm water (105 to 115 degrees)
Pinch of sugar
2 envelopes dry yeast (2 tablespoons)
2 cups lukewarm milk (scalded and cooled)
1/3 cup sugar
1/3 cup shortening or softened unsalted butter
1 tablespoon baking powder
2 teaspoons salt
1 egg

6 1/2 to 7 1/2 cups all-purpose flour
1/2 cup sugar
1 tablespoon plus 1 teaspoon cinnamon
1/4 cup (1/2 stick) unsalted butter, softened

CONFECTIONERS' SUGAR FROSTING
2 cups confectioners' sugar
2 tablespoons milk
1 teaspoon pure vanilla extract

EQUIPMENT NEEDED: Two 9×13-inch baking pans

To prepare the cinnamon rolls, mix the water and sugar in a large bowl. Sprinkle the yeast over the top and stir to dissolve. Let stand in a warm place to proof for 5 to 10 minutes or until the yeast swells and becomes bubbly. Add the milk, 1/3 cup sugar, the shortening, baking powder, salt, egg and 3 cups of the flour and beat until smooth. Stir in enough of the remaining flour to make a dough that is easy to handle. Knead on a well-floured surface for 8 to 10 minutes or until smooth and elastic. Place in a greased bowl, turning to coat the surface. Let rise, covered, in a warm draft-free place for 1 1/2 hours or until doubled in bulk. The dough is ready if an indentation remains when touched.

Mix 1/2 cup sugar and the cinnamon together. Punch down the dough. Divide the dough into two equal portions. Roll one portion at a time into a 10×12-inch rectangle. Spread each with the butter and sprinkle with the cinnamon-sugar. Roll up beginning at the 12-inch side and pinch the edge to seal. Stretch each to a uniform width and cut into twelve slices. Place twelve slices slightly apart in each of two greased 9×13-inch baking pans. Wrap each pan tightly with heavy-duty foil. Chill for 12 to 48 hours. Preheat the oven to 350 degrees. Bake, uncovered, for 30 to 35 minutes or until golden brown.

To prepare the frosting, combine the confectioners' sugar, milk and vanilla in a bowl and stir until smooth and of spreading consistency. Spread over the warm rolls.

Note: Our cinnamon rolls are made the day before, so all you need to do on Sunday morning is preheat the oven. If you plan to bake immediately instead of chilling the dough, let rise, uncovered, in a warm place for 30 minutes or until doubled in bulk and then bake as directed.

Variation: For Caramel Cinnamon Rolls, heat 2 cups packed brown sugar, 1 cup (2 sticks) unsalted butter, 1 teaspoon cinnamon and 3 tablespoons corn syrup in a small saucepan just until melted. Do not boil. Pour half the mixture into each of two baking pans and sprinkle each with 1 cup chopped pecans. Place the cinnamon rolls over the caramel mixture and continue with the recipe as directed.

Salads

Arugula with Watermelon and Feta Cheese, page 68

Arugula with Watermelon and Feta Cheese

SERVES 2

1 cup (1-inch) watermelon cubes
2 ounces firm feta cheese, crumbled
2 tablespoons balsamic vinegar
1/2 teaspoon freshly ground pepper, or to taste
1 tablespoon extra-virgin olive oil
2 cups arugula or mixed salad greens
Salt to taste
2 tablespoons chopped toasted almonds

Combine the watermelon, cheese, vinegar and pepper in a medium bowl. Macerate in the refrigerator for 15 minutes. Add the olive oil, arugula and salt and toss to mix. Sprinkle with the almonds and serve.

Note: A quick-and-easy salad for two made with the peppery, mustard flavor of arugula. Buy the freshest arugula available. It is highly perishable. Fresh strawberries or peaches may be used instead of the watermelon.

Summer Fruit Salad

SERVES 4 TO 6

1 cup (1-inch) fresh pineapple chunks
1 cup chopped fresh strawberries
1 kiwifruit, peeled and sliced
1 papaya, peeled and cut into 1/2-inch pieces
1/2 cup chopped red onion
1 jalapeño chile, seeded and finely chopped
1/4 cup chopped fresh cilantro or flat-leaf parsley
2 tablespoons fresh lime juice (about 1 lime)

Combine the pineapple, strawberries, kiwifruit, papaya, onion, jalapeño chile, cilantro and lime juice in a medium bowl and toss to mix. Chill, covered, for 1 hour or longer before serving.

Note: This refreshing salad is delicious alongside fish or pork, with tortilla chips, or just by itself.

Salads

Gala Apple and Pear Salad with Mustard Pear Vinaigrette

MUSTARD PEAR VINAIGRETTE
1/3 cup pear vinegar
1 tablespoon Dijon mustard
1 teaspoon sugar
1/8 to 1/4 teaspoon cinnamon, or to taste
1/4 teaspoon coarse salt
1/4 teaspoon freshly ground pepper
1/3 cup extra-virgin olive oil

SALAD
4 cups torn or chopped red leaf lettuce
4 cups torn or chopped romaine

1 bunch watercress, or 1 cup coarsely
   chopped arugula
1/4 cup chopped fresh flat-leaf parsley
1 red onion, thinly sliced
2 large Gala apples, cored and thinly sliced
1 ripe Bosc or Bartlett pear, peeled, cored and
   thinly sliced
1 cup chopped toasted walnuts or pecans
Salt and freshly ground pepper to taste

EQUIPMENT NEEDED: A food processor or electric blender

To prepare the vinaigrette, process the vinegar, Dijon mustard, sugar, cinnamon, salt and pepper in a food processor or electric blender until smooth. Add the olive oil in a slow steady stream, processing constantly until emulsified.

To prepare the salad, combine the red leaf lettuce, romaine, watercress, parsley, onion, apples, pear and walnuts in a large bowl. Sprinkle with salt and pepper. Drizzle with the vinaigrette and toss to coat.

Note: For a heartier salad, arrange thinly sliced strips of roasted or smoked chicken or leftover roast beef on top of the salad before serving. Pear vinegar is available at specialty markets.

Olive Oil

Extra-virgin olive oil must have less than one percent acidity. The taste, aroma, and color are all judged by experts of the European Economic Community who set the standard for all olive oils. A single, cold-press oil that is filtered to remove sediments and lighten color, olive oil may be used in any recipe calling for vegetable oil, even sweet batters. Just remember that it has a lower flash point than many other vegetable oils.

Mojito Salad with Honey Rum Dressing

SERVES 10

HONEY RUM DRESSING
1/2 cup canola oil
1/2 cup fresh lime juice (about 3 limes)
1/3 cup honey
1 tablespoon dark rum
3/4 teaspoon sea salt

SALAD
1/2 cup thinly sliced red onion halves
Juice of 1 lime
1 (8-ounce) jicama, peeled and julienned
1 English cucumber, thinly sliced (about 3 cups)
1/2 of (5-pound) seedless watermelon, cut into
    1-inch cubes
1 pound strawberries, cut into halves lengthwise
1/2 cup blueberries
1/3 cup lightly packed fresh mint leaves, chopped

To prepare the dressing, whisk the canola oil, lime juice, honey, rum and sea salt in a small bowl. Chill, covered, until serving time.

To prepare the salad, soak the onion in the lime juice in a small nonreactive bowl for 2 to 10 hours. Place the undrained onions in a large bowl. Add the jicama, cucumber, watermelon, strawberries, blueberries and mint. Pour the dressing over the top and toss to mix. Serve cold or at room temperature.

Note: A mandolin is helpful when preparing this colorful red, white, and blue salad that is wonderful for picnics.

Garden Fresh Salad with Tomato Poppy Seed Dressing

SERVES 8 TO 10

TOMATO POPPY SEED DRESSING
1 tablespoon poppy seeds
3 tablespoons herb vinegar, such as tarragon
    or rosemary
1 tablespoon tomato paste
2 teaspoons sugar
1/2 cup extra-virgin olive oil
Salt and freshly ground pepper to taste

SALAD
1 bunch baby arugula or spinach leaves
1 head green leaf lettuce, torn
1 head radicchio, chopped
1 1/2 cups grape tomato or cherry tomato halves
1 cup shredded carrots
1 cup fresh corn kernels
1 cup fresh peas
1/4 cup chopped scallions (white and green parts)
1/4 cup sliced almonds or pine nuts, toasted
1/4 cup chopped flat-leaf parsley
3 tablespoons chopped cilantro

To prepare the dressing, whisk the poppy seeds, vinegar, tomato paste, sugar, olive oil, salt and pepper in a small bowl. Chill, covered, until serving time.

To prepare the salad, combine the arugula, green leaf lettuce, radicchio, grape tomatoes, carrots, corn, peas, scallions, almonds, parsley and cilantro in a large bowl and toss to mix. Chill, covered, until serving time. Add the dressing just before serving and toss to coat.

Note: Make this salad when your garden is bursting with fresh herbs and vegetables. It is versatile enough to handle any combination of herbs you care to harvest.

Avocado and Tomatillo Salsa Crumble

SERVES 4

8 plum tomatoes, chopped (about 1 pound)
4 tomatillos, peeled and chopped
1/2 cup finely chopped red onion
2 tablespoons finely chopped flat-leaf parsley
1 tablespoon fresh lime juice
1/4 teaspoon salt
1/4 teaspoon freshly cracked pepper

2 avocados, sliced
Lime juice for brushing
2 small zucchini, thinly sliced
1/4 cup flat-leaf parsley, coarsely chopped
16 black olives, pitted
4 slices corn bread or 4 corn muffins, crumbled

Mix the tomatoes, tomatillos, onion, parsley, 1 tablespoon lime juice, the salt and pepper in a bowl. Brush the avocados with lime juice to prevent browning. Place the zucchini in a ring around each of four salad plates. Spoon the salsa in the center of each and spread to cover half the zucchini. Arrange the avocados on top of the salsa. Sprinkle with the parsley. Divide the olives among the plates and top with the corn bread.

Note: The flavor of tomatillos, also known as Mexican green tomatoes, has a hint of lemon, apple, and herbs. Their thin, papery husks indicate they are related to the cape gooseberry.

Grilled Chicories with Nasturtium Blossoms

SERVES 4

1/2 cup extra-virgin olive oil, walnut oil or
    pistachio oil
6 tablespoons red wine vinegar
1 tablespoon chopped fresh chives
Salt and freshly ground pepper to taste
1 head radicchio, cut into quarters

2 heads Belgian endive, cut into halves
1 head frisée (curly leaf endive),
    cut into quarters
1/4 cup chopped pistachios
Nasturtium blossoms for garnish

EQUIPMENT NEEDED: An outdoor grill or large grill pan

Whisk the olive oil, vinegar, chives, salt and pepper in a small bowl. Preheat an outdoor grill to medium-high. Brush the cut sides of the radicchio, endive and frisée with some of the vinaigrette. Marinate at room temperature for 15 minutes; drain. Place cut side down on a grill rack. Grill for 1 to 2 minutes or just until lightly seared. Grill only the cut sides, and grill the frisée last as it cooks the fastest. Arrange one of each chicory grilled side up on each of four serving plates. Drizzle with the remaining vinaigrette. Garnish each serving with some of the pistachios and nasturtium blossoms.

Note: A charcoal grill will give chicories even more flavor and aroma. If cooking indoors, heat a grill pan over medium-high heat. Place the chicories cut side down and grill until they begin to soften.

 Chicory

Chicory is a biennial herb that grows wild on roadsides in North America and Europe. Its lavender-colored flowers appear in early summer. Radicchio and witloof, known commonly as French or Belgian endive, are members of the genus, *Cichorium*. Their raw leaves add bite to a salad. Root chicory, *Cichorium intybus*, is used as a caffeine-free coffee substitute in Europe. When added to coffee, it is a New Orleans tradition.

Basil Corn Salad with
Green Beans and Cherry Tomatoes

1^1/2 pounds green beans, trimmed
Salt to taste
3 ears fresh corn, husks and silks removed
1 tablespoon extra-virgin olive oil
Freshly ground pepper to taste
1^1/2 cups cherry tomato halves (about 9 ounces)
1 large shallot, finely chopped
^{1}/3 cup lightly packed fresh basil leaves, chiffonade cut
3 tablespoons tarragon vinegar or white wine vinegar
^{1}/2 cup extra-virgin olive oil
Arugula or mixed greens (optional)

EQUIPMENT NEEDED: A large saucepan; an outdoor grill or large baking pan

Cook the green beans in boiling salted water in a large saucepan for 4 minutes or until tender-crisp. Rinse immediately with cold water to stop the cooking process. Drain and pat dry. (The green beans can be prepared 1 day in advance. Wrap and chill in the refrigerator.)

Preheat an outdoor grill to medium heat. Brush the corn on the cob with 1 tablespoon olive oil and sprinkle with salt and pepper. Place on a grill rack. Grill for 10 minutes or until brown in spots, turning occasionally. Remove from the heat to cool. (See Note.)

Cut the kernels from the corn cobs into a large bowl using a sharp knife. Add the green beans and tomatoes. Mix the shallot, basil and vinegar in a small bowl. Whisk in ^{1}/2 cup olive oil gradually. Season with salt and pepper. Add to the corn mixture and toss to mix. Serve alone or over arugula or mixed salad greens.

Note: Grilled corn gives this salad a nutty flavor. To roast the corn in the oven, preheat the oven to 425 degrees. Place the uncooked corn kernels and tomatoes in a large baking pan and drizzle with 2 tablespoons olive oil. Bake for 15 to 20 minutes or until roasted. Remove from the oven to cool. Continue with the recipe as above.

Sweet basil (*Ocimum basilicum*)

Mediterranean Salad with Eggplant, Bell Peppers and Mint

1/2 cup extra-virgin olive oil

3 tablespoons fresh lemon juice

1 teaspoon coarse sea salt

1/2 teaspoon freshly ground pepper

1 3/4 pounds eggplant (preferably long, narrow Japanese variety)

1 pound mixed red, green, orange and yellow bell peppers, cut into 1-inch pieces

1 cup cherry tomatoes, cut into halves

1/4 cup coarsely chopped mint leaves

1/4 cup coarsely chopped kalamata olives

2 tablespoons capers, chopped

1 garlic clove, minced

1/2 teaspoon ground sumac

1/2 teaspoon chopped fresh thyme

3 ounces feta cheese, crumbled (about 2/3 cup)

EQUIPMENT NEEDED: A large baking sheet

Preheat the oven to 450 degrees. Whisk the olive oil, lemon juice, salt and pepper in a bowl to make a vinaigrette. Chop the unpeeled eggplant into 1-inch pieces. Toss with 1/3 cup of the vinaigrette in a bowl. Arrange in a single layer on a large baking sheet. Bake for 30 minutes or until tender and golden brown around the edges, tossing occasionally. Let stand until slightly cool. (The eggplant can be warm, but should not be hot enough to melt the cheese or wilt the mint.)

Combine the eggplant, bell peppers, tomatoes and mint in a large bowl. Whisk the olives, capers, garlic, sumac, thyme and cheese into the remaining vinaigrette. Pour over the eggplant mixture and toss to coat. Serve immediately or within a few hours. It will hold up all day.

 ## Sumac

The fruity, astringent flavor of sumac complements this salad to make it crisp, juicy, and piquant—perfect for a hot summer day. Sumac comes from the dark berries of a bush that grows wild in parts of the Mediterranean region and can be found in specialty spice stores or international markets.

Lentil Salad with Fresh Vegetables and Curry Dressing

CURRY DRESSING
1/4 cup extra-virgin olive oil
1/4 cup balsamic vinegar
3 tablespoons fresh lemon juice (about 1 medium lemon)
4 teaspoons St. Louis Herb Society Curry Powder (page 49) or store-bought equivalent
2 garlic cloves, crushed
Salt and freshly ground pepper to taste

SALAD
6 cups low-sodium chicken broth (preferably homemade)
2 cups dried lentils, rinsed and drained
Assortment of fresh vegetables, such as blanched chilled broccoli or cauliflower florets, a mixture of chopped red, green, orange or yellow bell peppers, grated carrots, chopped zucchini, sliced celery, chopped scallions and/or sliced red onions
3 tablespoons chopped fresh flat-leaf parsley

EQUIPMENT NEEDED: A large saucepan; a colander

To prepare the dressing, whisk the olive oil, vinegar, lemon juice, curry powder and garlic in a small bowl. Sprinkle with salt and pepper.

To prepare the salad, bring the broth to a boil in a large saucepan. Add the lentils. Simmer gently for 20 to 25 minutes or just until tender. Drain in a colander and rinse with cold water to stop the cooking process. Drain thoroughly and place in a large bowl. Add the dressing and assorted fresh vegetables and toss to mix. Chill, covered, for 4 hours or longer. Add the parsley just before serving and toss to mix.

Note: Brown or green lentils are acceptable for this dish, but French or black lentils are preferred. They are smaller, creamier, and more attractive.

Middle Eastern Garbanzo Salad

1/4 cup extra-virgin olive oil
1 cup finely chopped yellow onion
2 tablespoons coarsely chopped fresh thyme
1/2 cup coarsely chopped red bell pepper
1/2 cup dark raisins

2 (15-ounce) cans garbanzo beans (chickpeas), rinsed and drained
1/2 teaspoon salt
1/2 teaspoon ground sumac (optional)
1/4 cup tarragon vinegar or other herb vinegar
1/4 cup fresh lemon juice

EQUIPMENT NEEDED: A medium saucepan

Heat the olive oil in a medium saucepan. Add the onion and thyme. Cook, covered, over low heat for 25 minutes or until the onion is tender and lightly colored. Add the bell pepper. Cook for 5 minutes. Add the raisins and beans. Cook for 5 minutes, stirring occasionally. Do not overcook, or the beans will become mushy. Spoon into a large bowl and sprinkle with the salt and sumac. Stir in the vinegar and lemon juice. Let cool to room temperature. Chill, covered, for 24 hours or longer. Bring to room temperature before serving.

Herb and Roasted Pepper Salad

2 large red bell peppers, cut into halves lengthwise (see Note)
2 large yellow bell peppers, cut into halves lengthwise (see Note)
2 large orange bell peppers, cut into halves lengthwise (see Note)
1/3 cup sliced pitted black olives
2 tablespoons sliced scallions
2 garlic cloves, minced

2 tablespoons drained capers
2 tablespoons chopped fresh basil leaves
2 tablespoons chopped fresh oregano
3 tablespoons extra-virgin olive oil
2 tablespoons balsamic vinegar
1/4 teaspoon freshly ground pepper
Lettuce of choice
1/4 cup crumbled feta cheese for garnish

EQUIPMENT NEEDED: A large baking sheet

Preheat the oven to 400 degrees. Roast the bell peppers on a large baking sheet for 45 minutes or until the skins are blackened. Place in a nonrecyled brown paper bag or sealable plastic bag and seal the bag. Let stand for 15 minutes. Remove the skins from the bell peppers. Cut the bell peppers into strips.

Combine the bell peppers, olives, scallions, garlic, capers, basil, oregano, olive oil, balsamic vinegar and pepper in a medium bowl and toss to mix. Chill, covered, for 3 hours or longer. Serve on lettuce-lined serving plates and garnish with the feta cheese.

Note: This is wonderful simply served on lettuce, but it also makes a delicious appetizer as a topping for bruschetta. It may also be served on an antipasto tray or in panini. The fresh bell peppers may be substituted with one 24-ounce jar roasted red peppers, drained and cut into strips.

Fennel Slaw

1 large fennel bulb with feathery green tops
1 small carrot, peeled and julienned
1 apple, cut into 1-inch pieces
1 pear, peeled and chopped

1/2 cup dried cherries, dried cranberries or
dried blueberries
1/2 cup Slaw Dressing (recipe follows)

Cut the outer stalks and feathery greens from the fennel bulb, reserving the feathery greens. Cut the bulb into quarters. Cut away the core and discard. Coarsely chop the fennel bulb quarters. Rinse and pat dry. Place in a medium bowl.

Chop enough of the reserved feathery greens to yield 2 tablespoons. Add to the chopped fennel with the carrot, apple, pear and dried cherries. Add the dressing and toss to combine. Serve immediately

Note: When shopping for fennel, look for clean, crisp bulbs without any brown spots and having bright green tops. Grocers often label fennel as sweet anise, Florence fennel, or finocchio. The leftover greens are good in soups.

Slaw Dressing

1 cup mayonnaise or mayonnaise-type
salad dressing
1/3 cup apple cider vinegar
1/3 cup sugar

1 1/2 teaspoons salt
1 1/2 teaspoons fresh dill, minced
3/4 teaspoon fines herbes
Freshly ground pepper to taste

Combine the mayonnaise, vinegar, sugar, salt, dill, fines herbes and pepper in a small bowl and mix well. Chill, covered, until serving time.

Fines Herbes
A classic in French cuisine, *fines herbes* are made of equal amounts of very finely chopped chervil, chives, parsley, and tarragon. Unlike bouquet garni that is made of pungent herbs and requires cooking to release their flavors, these "fine herbs" quickly lose their flavor, so they should be added to a dish just before serving. Salad burnet, cress, cicely, lemon balm, marjoram, or savory often is added to the classic mixture.

Napa Cabbage and Papaya Slaw with Ginger Vinaigrette

GINGER VINAIGRETTE
1/4 cup canola oil
2 tablespoons tarragon vinegar, white balsamic
    vinegar or white wine vinegar
1 tablespoon honey
1 teaspoon freshly grated gingerroot, or
    1/2 teaspoon ground ginger
Salt and freshly ground pepper to taste

SALAD
1 small head napa cabbage, thinly shredded
1 cup (1-inch) fresh papaya cubes
1/2 cup chopped red bell pepper
1/3 cup chopped red onion
1 jalapeño chile, seeded and finely chopped
4 slices bacon, crisp-cooked and crumbled
1/4 cup chopped or whole toasted sunflower
    seeds or pistachios for garnish

To prepare the vinaigrette, mix the canola oil, vinegar, honey, gingerroot, salt and pepper in a small bowl or a jar with a lid. Chill, covered, until serving time.

To prepare the salad, combine the cabbage, papaya, bell pepper, onion, jalapeño chile and bacon in a medium bowl and toss to mix. Add the vinaigrette and toss to coat. Garnish with the sunflower seeds.

Note: Napa cabbage is a milder, sweeter, and more delicate alternative to green cabbage. It has a hint of celery flavor.

Sweet Potato Salad with Kielbasa

6 sweet potatoes (about 3 pounds)
Salt to taste
1 pound kielbasa or similar smoked sausage,
    casings removed
1 tablespoon extra-virgin olive oil
1 red onion, chopped

3 tablespoons extra-virgin olive oil
1/3 cup balsamic vinegar
3 tablespoons German-style prepared mustard
Pinch of sugar
1/2 cup chopped flat-leaf parsley
Freshly ground pepper to taste

EQUIPMENT NEEDED: A large stockpot; a colander; a medium skillet

Cook the unpeeled whole sweet potatoes in boiling salted water in a large stockpot until fork tender. Drain in a colander and let stand until cool enough to handle. Peel the sweet potatoes. Cut into bite-size pieces and place in a large bowl.

Brown the sausage in 1 tablespoon olive oil in a medium skillet. Cut into bite-size pieces. Add the sausage and onion to the sweet potatoes.

Whisk 3 tablespoons olive oil, the vinegar, mustard and sugar in a small bowl. Pour over the sweet potato mixture and toss gently. Sprinkle with the parsley, salt and pepper. Serve warm or at room temperature.

Note: A hearty and heartwarming dish perfect for a chilly evening, it can be served as a side dish or main course.

Grilled Flank Steak and Cucumber Salad

1 beef flank steak, scored diagonally
^{1}/4 cup soy sauce
^{1}/4 cup sweet soy sauce or stir-fry sauce
1 tablespoon hoisin sauce
2 tablespoons rice wine vinegar
1 garlic clove, chopped
1 teaspoon grated fresh gingerroot
1 tablespoon finely chopped fresh lemon grass

^{1}/4 cup water
5 ounces arugula
1 English cucumber
2 scallions, chopped
2 tablespoons chopped flat-leaf parsley
2 tablespoons white wine vinegar
1 tablespoon extra-virgin olive oil
Cracked pepper to taste

EQUIPMENT NEEDED: An outdoor grill

Place the steak in a 1-gallon sealable plastic bag. Mix the soy sauce, sweet soy sauce, hoisin sauce, rice wine vinegar, garlic, gingerroot, lemon grass and water in a small bowl. Pour over the steak and seal the bag. Marinate in the refrigerator for 3 to 10 hours, turning occasionally.

Preheat the grill. Drain the steak, discarding the marinade. Pat the steak dry and place on a grill rack. Grill to 145 degrees on a meat thermometer for medium-rare. Remove from the heat and let rest for 10 minutes. Cut across the grain into thin slices.

Divide the arugula among four salad plates. Cut the cucumber into strips lengthwise using a vegetable peeler. Combine the cucumber strips, scallions, parsley, white wine vinegar and olive oil in a bowl and toss to mix. Place the steak on the arugula and top with the cucumber mixture. Sprinkle with cracked pepper.

Note: Simply put, grilled flank steak and summer just go together. Ours is easy to prepare and packed with flavor.

 ## Herbed Croutons

Make your own quick-and-easy croutons by adding ^{1}/2 teaspoon crushed dried rosemary, ^{1}/2 teaspoon garlic powder, and ^{1}/4 teaspoon dried thyme to ^{1}/2 cup (1 stick) melted butter in a bowl. Add 2 cups cubed dry bread and mix well. Spread on a baking sheet and bake in a 350-degree oven for 15 minutes or until brown, stirring occasionally. Serve on soup or in a salad.

Green Bean and Grilled Salmon Salad with Herb Vinaigrette

HERB VINAIGRETTE
2 tablespoons herbal vinegar, such as tarragon
   or lemon
2 tablespoons extra-virgin olive oil
2 tablespoons fresh lemon juice
1 teaspoon water
3 tablespoons chopped fresh flat-leaf parsley
2 tablespoons finely chopped fresh basil leaves
1/4 teaspoon salt
1/4 teaspoon freshly ground pepper

SALAD
1 pound fresh green beans, trimmed and
   cut into halves
Salt to taste
8 ounces boneless skinless grilled salmon,
   cut into chunks
1 small white onion, thinly sliced and
   separated into rings
1 small or 1/2 medium red bell pepper,
   cut into 1/2-inch pieces
2 cups baby salad greens or shredded lettuce
6 cherry tomatoes or grape tomatoes,
   cut into halves for garnish

EQUIPMENT NEEDED: A large saucepan; a colander

To prepare the vinaigrette, whisk the vinegar, olive oil, lemon juice, water, parsley, basil, salt and pepper in a small bowl. Chill, covered, until serving time.

To prepare the salad, cook the green beans in boiling salted water in a large saucepan just until tender. Drain in a colander and immediately plunge into ice water. Drain and pat dry. Combine the green beans, salmon, onion and bell pepper in a 1-gallon sealable plastic bag. Add the vinaigrette and seal the bag, turning to coat. Chill for 2 to 10 hours. Serve on the baby salad greens and garnish with the cherry tomatoes.

Note: A lovely salad to make ahead and serve when you are ready. For a quick lunch or supper, substitute grilled salmon with precooked salmon from a pouch.

Tuna Salad

1 cup balsamic vinegar
8 ounces cooked fresh tuna, flaked
1/2 cup chopped black olives
1/2 cup chopped green olives
1/4 cup capers, drained and rinsed
1 teaspoon pressed garlic

1/2 cup chopped sweet basil leaves
1/2 cup chopped flat-leaf parsley
Freshly ground pepper to taste
1/4 cup (about) extra-virgin olive oil
Crusty bread, sliced tomatoes or salad greens

EQUIPMENT NEEDED: A small saucepan

Simmer the vinegar in a small saucepan until reduced to 1/4 cup, watching carefully to prevent burning. Remove from the heat and set aside. Combine the tuna, olives, capers, garlic, basil, parsley and pepper in a bowl and mix with a fork. Add enough olive oil to reach the desired consistency. Pile onto crusty bread, tomatoes or salad greens and drizzle with the vinegar reduction.

Note: Our unique Mediterranean-style tuna salad is brimming with herbs.

Savory Chicken Salad

2 whole chicken breasts, cut into halves
3 quarts (12 cups) water
Salt to taste
1 carrot, peeled
5 or 6 ribs celery
1 large fresh bay leaf, or 2 small fresh
    bay leaves
6 whole black peppercorns
16 small new potatoes, cut into halves
1 cup chopped scallions
1/3 cup olive oil

1/3 cup vegetable oil
1/3 cup red wine vinegar
1 tablespoon fresh lemon juice
1 tablespoon chopped fresh basil leaves
1 tablespoon chopped fresh dill
1 tablespoon chopped fresh mint leaves
1 teaspoon grated gingerroot
1 teaspoon sugar
2 teaspoons salt
Freshly ground pepper to taste
Fresh lettuce or salad greens

EQUIPMENT NEEDED: A large stockpot; a colander

Place the chicken in a large stockpot. Add the water and salt to taste. Bring to a boil. Reduce the heat and simmer, partially covered, for 10 minutes. Add the carrot, one rib of the celery, the bay leaf, peppercorns and potatoes. Simmer, covered, for 20 minutes or until the chicken is cooked through. Remove the potatoes and set aside to cool. Cool the chicken in the poaching liquid.

Chop the remaining celery to measure about 2 cups. Remove the chicken from the poaching liquid, discarding the liquid and solids. Tear the chicken into bite-size pieces, discarding the skin and bones. Combine the chicken, potatoes, scallions and 2 cups celery in a medium bowl and toss to mix.

Whisk the olive oil, vegetable oil, vinegar, lemon juice, basil, dill, mint, gingerroot , sugar and 2 teaspoons salt together in a small bowl. Pour over the chicken mixture and toss to mix. Chill, covered, for 2 to 10 hours.

To serve, drain the chicken mixture in a colander and place in a serving bowl. Sprinkle with pepper. Serve with bite-size pieces of the lettuce mixed in or on a bed of salad greens.

Note: A surprising change from the usual, our chicken salad is loaded with herbs and is at its best after chilling overnight. Always tear, never cut the chicken so that the dressing can seep into its crevices.

Pastas & Grains

Barley Risotto with Thyme and Portobello Mushrooms

2 tablespoons olive oil
8 ounces portobello mushrooms, wiped clean
    and cut into 1-inch pieces
2 garlic cloves, chopped
1 tablespoon chopped fresh thyme
2 tablespoons olive oil
1 onion, coarsely chopped
10 (about) purple sage leaves, coarsely chopped
4$^{1}/_{2}$ cups chicken broth (preferably homemade)

1 cup pearl barley, rinsed
$^{1}/_{4}$ teaspoon freshly grated nutmeg
$^{1}/_{8}$ teaspoon cinnamon
$^{1}/_{2}$ cup white wine
$^{1}/_{2}$ cup golden raisins
Salt and freshly ground pepper to taste
2 tablespoons butter, cut into cubes
2 tablespoons chopped fresh flat-leaf parsley

EQUIPMENT NEEDED: A large heavy saucepan; a medium saucepan

Heat 2 tablespoons olive oil in a large heavy saucepan over medium-high heat. Add the mushrooms and sauté for 5 minutes. Add the garlic and thyme and sauté for 1 minute. Remove the mushroom mixture to a bowl.

Reduce the heat to medium. Add 2 tablespoons olive oil and the onion to the pan drippings in the saucepan. Sauté for 5 minutes. Add the sage and sauté for 5 minutes or until the onion is soft.

Bring the broth to a boil in a medium saucepan; reduce the heat. Cover and simmer gently. Stir the barley, nutmeg and cinnamon into the onion mixture. Cook over medium-high heat for 1 minute, stirring constantly to coat the barley evenly with the oil. Add the wine. Cook for 5 minutes or until the wine is nearly evaporated, stirring constantly. Add the hot broth $^{1}/_{2}$ cup at a time, stirring constantly and cooking over medium heat until the broth is absorbed after each addition. The total cooking time for all the broth to become absorbed and the barley to become tender will be about 45 minutes. Stir in the mushroom mixture and raisins. Cook for a few minutes longer or until the risotto reaches the desired consistency. Sprinkle with salt and pepper. Stir in the butter. Serve immediately and garnish each serving with the parsley.

Note: This savory and sweet side dish is a unique change from the usual arborio rice risotto and is perfect with pork or chicken.

Purple sage (*Salvia officinalis* 'Purpurascens')

Vegetables

Braised Celery with Chervil and French Thyme, page 100

White Asparagus with Lime Hollandaise Sauce   SERVES 4

2 pounds white asparagus
1/2 cup (1 stick) unsalted butter
3 egg yolks
3 tablespoons fresh lime juice
2 teaspoons finely chopped lemon verbena

1 tablespoon finely chopped flat-leaf parsley
3 drops of Tabasco sauce
Freshly ground sea salt to taste
1/2 teaspoon white pepper

EQUIPMENT NEEDED: A medium saucepan; a small saucepan; a food processor

Snap off the woody ends of the asparagus spears. Use a vegetable peeler to strip off the outer layer of each spear from just below the tip to the end of the spear. Cook in gently boiling water in a medium saucepan for 10 minutes or until tender. Drain and place in a warm serving dish.

Melt the butter in a small saucepan until hot and bubbly. Pulse the egg yolks, lime juice, lemon verbena, parsley, Tabasco sauce, salt and white pepper once or twice in a food processor until blended. Drizzle the butter through the feed tube, processing constantly for 10 seconds or until emulsified. Drizzle over the asparagus.

Note: Our unique version of hollandaise sauce is perfect and does not overpower the delicate flavor of the white asparagus. If you are concerned about using raw egg yolks, use eggs pasteurized in their shells or an equivalent amount of egg yolk substitute.

Green Beans with Amaretti Herb Crust   SERVES 4 TO 6

1 pound fresh green beans
Salt to taste
1/2 cup panko (Japanese bread crumbs) or fresh
   bread crumbs
2 tablespoons finely crushed amaretti
   (Italian almond cookies)
2 tablespoons freshly grated Parmigiano-
   Reggiano cheese

1 tablespoon chopped fresh flat-leaf parsley
1 tablespoon chopped fresh marjoram
1/2 teaspoon (scant) coarse salt
Freshly ground pepper to taste
2 tablespoons butter, melted
Lemon wedges

EQUIPMENT NEEDED: A medium saucepan; a medium baking dish

Snap off the ends of the green beans. Snap the green beans into halves and remove the strings. Blanch the green beans in boiling salted water in a medium saucepan for 2 to 3 minutes. Drain and plunge immediately into ice water to stop the cooking process. Drain and let stand until dry.

Toss the panko, amaretti, cheese, parsley, marjoram, 1/2 teaspoon salt and pepper to taste together in a small bowl. Add the butter and mix well.

Preheat the oven to 425 degrees. Place the green beans in a buttered medium baking dish and top with the panko mixture. Bake for 15 to 20 minutes or until heated through and the crust is golden brown. Serve with lemon wedges and pepper to taste.

Note: Green beans can be blanched in advance and baked just before serving.

Carrot Wreath with Caramelized Brussels Sprouts   SERVES 8

CARROT WREATH
2 pounds carrots, peeled and cut into quarters
1 garlic clove, crushed
Salt to taste
1 1/2 cups panko (Japanese bread crumbs)
1 cup (4 ounces) shredded sharp
    Cheddar cheese
1 cup milk
1/2 cup (1 stick) butter, melted
1/3 cup grated onion
1 tablespoon chopped fresh flat-leaf parsley
1 teaspoon (heaping) chopped fresh thyme

1 teaspoon sea salt
1 teaspoon freshly ground black pepper
1/2 teaspoon cayenne pepper
3 eggs

CARAMELIZED BRUSSELS SPROUTS
3 pounds fresh Brussels sprouts
1/2 cup (1 stick) unsalted butter
1 tablespoon sugar
1 tablespoon chopped fresh marjoram
Coarse salt and freshly ground pepper to taste

EQUIPMENT NEEDED: A medium saucepan; a 6-cup ring mold; a large skillet

To prepare the carrot wreath, place the carrots and garlic in a medium saucepan and cover with salted cold water. Bring to a boil. Reduce the heat and cook until the carrots are tender; drain. Place in a medium bowl. Mash the carrot mixture gently. Add the panko, cheese, milk, butter, onion, parsley, thyme, 1 teaspoon salt, the black pepper and cayenne pepper and mix well. Beat the eggs in a small bowl until light and fluffy. Fold into the carrot mixture. Preheat the oven to 350 degrees. Spread the carrot mixture evenly into a greased 6-cup ring mold. Bake for 40 to 45 minutes or until a wooden pick inserted in the center comes out clean.

To prepare the sprouts, remove the tough outer leaves of the sprouts. Trim the stems and score each by making a small "x" with a paring knife. Steam until the sprouts are tender-crisp. Melt the butter in a large skillet over medium-high heat. Stir in the sugar. Add the steamed sprouts and sauté for 3 minutes. Reduce the heat to medium-low. Sauté for 15 minutes or until caramelized, brown and crispy, watching carefully to prevent overbrowning. Add the marjoram, salt and pepper.

To serve, unmold the carrot ring onto a warm serving platter. Fill the center of the ring with the sprouts and arrange any remaining sprouts around the edge of the ring.

Note: Serve on a silver tray and garnish with fresh cranberries and sprigs of fresh parsley for a dramatic and colorful display for your holiday party buffet.

Seasoned Salt

Mix 1 cup salt, 2 tablespoons paprika, 2 tablespoons dried parsley, 1 tablespoon dried chives, 1 tablespoon dried thyme, 1 tablespoon dried winter savory, 1 teaspoon dried minced garlic, 1/2 teaspoon dried marjoram, 1/2 teaspoon cayenne pepper, 1/2 teaspoon cracked black pepper, and 1/2 teaspoon white pepper in a bowl. Store in airtight container for up to six months.

Tarragon Carrots

SERVES 4

6 carrots, peeled
Salt to taste
2 cups cold water

2 tablespoons unsalted butter
1 tablespoon chopped fresh tarragon
Freshly ground pepper to taste

EQUIPMENT NEEDED: A medium saucepan

Cut the carrots into quarters and then cut into thin slices. Place in a medium saucepan and cover with salted cold water. Bring to a boil. Reduce the heat. Simmer until the carrots are tender-crisp; drain. Return the carrots to the saucepan and add the butter, tarragon, salt and pepper and mix until coated. Cook over low heat until tender. Remove from the heat and let stand for 5 minutes to allow the carrots to absorb the tarragon flavor.

Note: This simple dish is quite simply delicious.

Braised Celery with Chervil and French Thyme

SERVES 4

2 tablespoons unsalted butter
8 ribs celery, strings removed and celery
    cut into 3-inch pieces
1 cup chicken broth (preferably homemade)

1 tablespoon chopped fresh flat-leaf parsley
2 teaspoons chopped fresh chervil
2 teaspoons chopped fresh French thyme
Salt to taste

EQUIPMENT NEEDED: A medium skillet

Melt the butter in a medium skillet over medium heat. Add the celery and stir to coat. Add the broth, parsley, chervil and thyme. Bring to a boil; reduce the heat. Simmer for 5 minutes or until the celery starts to soften but is not mushy. Sprinkle with salt. Remove the celery with a slotted spoon to a serving dish and serve warm.

 ## Chervil and French Thyme
With a faint taste of licorice, chervil is often referred to as the "gourmet parsley" because of its lacy leaves and more delicate flavor. It is especially good with vegetables. French thyme has more flavor and is sweeter than English thyme and should be part of every herb garden.

Cauliflower Gratin with Herbed Mornay Sauce

SERVES 8 TO 10

HERBED MORNAY SAUCE
1/4 cup all-purpose flour
1 teaspoon herbes de Provence (page 108)
1 teaspoon dry mustard
1 teaspoon white pepper
1/2 teaspoon cayenne pepper
1/4 cup (1/2 stick) unsalted butter
1 1/2 cups milk
1/2 cup (2 ounces) freshly grated
    Parmesan cheese
1/2 cup (2 ounces) shredded Gruyère cheese
1/2 cup heavy cream or half-and-half

CAULIFLOWER GRATIN
1 large head cauliflower, trimmed and
    cut into florets
2 tablespoons salt
1 cup (4 ounces) shredded Gruyère cheese
1 cup fresh sourdough bread crumbs
2 tablespoons butter
1/2 cup (2 ounces) freshly grated
    Parmesan cheese

EQUIPMENT NEEDED: A medium saucepan; a medium stockpot; a 2-quart baking dish

To prepare the sauce, mix the flour, herbes de Provence, dry mustard, white pepper and cayenne pepper in a small bowl. Melt the butter in a medium saucepan over medium-low heat. Whisk in the flour mixture until combined. Cook for 2 minutes, stirring constantly; do not allow to brown. Whisk in the milk gradually. Cook until the sauce thickens and comes to a low boil, stirring constantly. Add the Parmesan cheese and Gruyère cheese and cook until melted. Remove from the heat. Whisk in the cream.

To prepare the gratin, place the cauliflower and salt in cold water in a medium stockpot. Bring to a boil. Reduce the heat and cook until tender. Drain the cauliflower and place in a greased 2-quart baking dish. Preheat the oven to 375 degrees. Pour the sauce over the cauliflower to cover. Sprinkle with the Gruyère cheese and bread crumbs. Dot with the butter and top with the Parmesan cheese. Bake for 15 to 20 minutes or until brown and bubbly.

Note: Creamy, rich, and delicately kissed with herbs, our version of mornay sauce does not overpower the flavor of the cauliflower.

St. Louis Herb Society   *101*

Caponata

3/4 cup (or more) olive oil
3 pounds eggplant, peeled and cut into 1-inch pieces
1 large green bell pepper, cut into 1-inch pieces
1 large red bell pepper, cut into 1-inch pieces
2 yellow onions, chopped
2 garlic cloves, minced
18 ounces grape tomatoes
1/2 of (14-ounce) can diced tomatoes
1 tablespoon crushed fennel seeds
1 teaspoon chopped fresh rosemary
1 teaspoon herbes de Provence (page 108)
1/3 cup red wine vinegar
1/2 cup chopped fresh flat-leaf parsley
1/2 cup pitted kalamata olives, chopped
1/2 cup thickly sliced pimento-stuffed green olives
2 tablespoons sugar
2 tablespoons drained capers
2 tablespoons tomato paste
Sea salt and freshly ground pepper to taste
3 ounces pine nuts, toasted

EQUIPMENT NEEDED: A large heavy skillet or Dutch oven

Combine the olive oil, eggplant, bell peppers, onions, garlic, grape tomatoes, diced tomatoes, fennel seeds, rosemary and herbs de Provence in a large heavy skillet or Dutch oven. Cook over medium heat for 20 to 30 minutes or until the eggplant is tender, stirring occasionally. Add the vinegar, parsley, olives, sugar, capers, tomato paste, salt and pepper and reduce the heat. Simmer, covered, for 15 minutes. Stir in the pine nuts and serve warm.

Note: Caponata is a versatile dish with a bittersweet sauce that can be served warm, cold, or anything in between. It only improves with age, so chill leftovers and use them for bruschetta appetizers or add to green salads for extra zing.

Wild Mushroom Tart with Herbs and Dry Vermouth

1 (1-crust) pie pastry	1 tablespoon chopped fresh flat-leaf parsley
1 tablespoon unsalted butter	Coarse salt and freshly ground pepper to taste
1 pound assorted exotic mushrooms, stems removed and caps sliced	3 tablespoons unsalted butter
	3 tablespoons all-purpose flour
2 shallots, finely chopped	1 cup half-and-half
1/4 cup dry vermouth	1/8 teaspoon freshly grated nutmeg
1 tablespoon chopped fresh marjoram	1/2 cup (2 ounces) shredded Gruyère cheese

EQUIPMENT NEEDED: A 10-inch tart pan with removable bottom; a medium skillet; a medium saucepan

Preheat the oven to 375 degrees. Line a 10-inch tart pan with the pastry, trimming the edge. Bake for 15 to 20 minutes or until golden brown. Remove from the oven to cool. Reduce the oven temperature to 350 degrees.

Melt 1 tablespoon butter in a medium skillet over medium-high heat. Add the mushrooms and shallots. Sauté until the mushrooms are wilted and moisture appears in the bottom of the skillet. Stir in the vermouth. Cook for 2 minutes. Remove from the heat. Add the marjoram, parsley, salt and pepper.

Melt 3 tablespoons butter in a medium saucepan over medium heat. Stir in the flour. Cook for 2 minutes, stirring constantly. Add the half-and-half gradually, stirring constantly. Cook until the sauce is thickened and just comes to a boil, stirring constantly. Stir in the nutmeg and remove from the heat. Stir in the mushroom mixture. Pour into the baked tart shell. Sprinkle with the cheese.

Bake for 25 minutes or until bubbly and golden brown on top. Remove from the oven. Let stand for 20 minutes before serving.

Note: This rich and elegant tart makes a perfect companion for meat.

 ## Nutmeg and Mace

Nutmeg and mace come from a large evergreen tree cultivated in the West Indies. The nutmeg portion is the seed kernel inside the fruit pulp, and mace is the lacy covering between the kernel and the pulp. Nutmeg stays fresher longer when kept whole and should be grated as needed. One whole nutmeg equals two to three teaspoons of ground nutmeg. Mace, considered a premium spice, is laid out flat and becomes crimson-colored when dry.

Parsnips and Carrots with Herbs

SERVES 4 TO 6

1 pound parsnips
1 pound carrots
Salt and freshly ground pepper to taste
1/4 cup (1/2 stick) unsalted butter
1/4 cup packed brown sugar

1 teaspoon dried basil
1 teaspoon dried rosemary
1 teaspoon dried thyme
Pinch of ground cumin
1 tablespoon chopped fresh flat-leaf parsley

EQUIPMENT NEEDED: A medium baking dish; a small saucepan

Preheat the oven to 325 degrees. Peel the parsnips and carrots. Cut each diagonally into slices 1/2 inch thick. Spread in a medium baking dish and sprinkle with salt and pepper.

Heat the butter and brown sugar in a small saucepan over medium heat, stirring until the sugar dissolves. Stir in the basil, rosemary, thyme and cumin. Pour over the vegetables. Bake for 1 hour, basting occasionally with the pan drippings to coat the vegetables. Sprinkle with the parsley and serve.

Note: When summer is past and your herbs are dried and stored, use them to slow cook these deliciously sweet root vegetables.

Potato, Scallion and Herb Gratin

SERVES 6

2 pounds baking potatoes, peeled and sliced
    1/16 inch thick
1 cup crumbled Gorgonzola cheese
1/2 cup chicken broth (preferably homemade)
2 tablespoons finely chopped scallions
    (white and light green parts)

1 tablespoon all-purpose flour
1 tablespoon chopped fresh marjoram
1 tablespoon chopped fresh oregano
1 tablespoon chopped fresh flat-leaf parsley
1 cup (4 ounces) shredded Swiss cheese
1 teaspoon paprika

EQUIPMENT NEEDED: A 1 1/2-quart baking dish

Preheat the oven to 350 degrees. Combine the potatoes, Gorgonzola cheese, broth, scallions, flour, marjoram, oregano and parsley in a large bowl and mix well. Spoon into a greased 1 1/2-quart baking dish. Sprinkle with the Swiss cheese and paprika. Bake, covered with foil, for 30 minutes. Increase the oven temperature to 450 degrees. Bake, uncovered, for 15 to 18 minutes or until brown on top. Let stand for 10 minutes before serving.

Note: Abundant with creamy cheeses, this side dish is best served with full-flavored meats such as beef, lamb, or ham.

Potato

The potato is not officially an herb. It is a member of the poisonous nightshade family. As such, one needs to be mindful of its potential for danger. Never eat anything green from the potato, as this is considered poisonous. Leaves, stems, and any green portions on the potato itself should always be discarded. The notion that most of the nutrients are found in the skin is legend. The skin does contain about one-half of a potato's *fiber*, but more than half of the *nutrients* lie within the potato itself.

Rosemary Sweet Potatoes with Toasted Pine Nuts

2 pounds sweet potatoes, peeled and cut into 1 1/2-inch pieces
2 tablespoons olive oil
2 tablespoons balsamic vinegar
2 tablespoons chopped fresh rosemary
Salt and freshly ground pepper to taste
1/4 cup toasted pine nuts

EQUIPMENT NEEDED: A medium baking dish

Preheat the oven to 375 degrees. Place the sweet potatoes in a medium baking dish. Add the olive oil, vinegar and rosemary and toss to coat. Sprinkle with salt and pepper. Bake for 45 minutes, stirring once or twice. Remove from the oven. Sprinkle with the pine nuts just before serving. Serve warm or at room temperature.

Spinach Gratin

10 ounces fresh spinach
4 ounces feta cheese, crumbled
1 egg, lightly beaten
1/4 teaspoon crumbled dried oregano
1 1/2 teaspoons lemon juice
2/3 cup panko (Japanese bread crumbs)
2 tablespoons unsalted butter, melted

EQUIPMENT NEEDED: A large saucepan; a 1 1/2-quart baking dish

Preheat the oven to 425 degrees. Rinse the spinach and remove the thick back veins. Place the undrained spinach in a large saucepan. Cook for 3 to 5 minutes or until wilted; drain well.

Combine the drained spinach, cheese, egg, oregano, lemon juice and 1 1/2 tablespoons of the panko in a bowl and mix well. Spoon into a 1 1/2-quart baking dish. Mix the remaining panko with the butter in a bowl. Sprinkle over the spinach mixture. Bake for 15 minutes or until the top is golden brown.

Butternut Squash with Pumpkin Seeds

SERVES 6

1 butternut squash
2 tablespoons olive oil
1/4 cup chopped fresh garlic chives, or chives
　　with 1 garlic clove, crushed

3 tablespoons coarsely chopped fresh marjoram
2 tablespoons toasted pumpkin seeds
1/2 teaspoon salt
1/4 teaspoon white pepper

EQUIPMENT NEEDED: A 10×15-inch baking pan; a large skillet

Preheat the oven to 375 degrees. Cut the squash into halves and remove the seeds. Place the squash cut side up in a 10×15-inch baking pan. Bake for about 30 minutes or until tender but not mushy. Remove from the oven. Let stand until cool to the touch. Scoop out the squash and cut into 1 1/2-inch pieces.

Heat the olive oil in a large skillet. Add the squash and garlic chives. Cook until the garlic chives begin to wilt. Add the marjoram, pumpkin seeds, salt and white pepper. Cook until heated through, stirring until the squash is well coated. Serve immediately.

Zucchini and Leek Pancakes with Fresh Tomatoes

MAKES 12 TO 15

1 1/2 pounds ripe tomatoes, peeled, seeded
　　and chopped
2 pounds zucchini, unpeeled and
　　coarsely shredded
2 leeks, grated (white portion only)
1 1/2 teaspoons coarse salt
2 eggs, lightly beaten
1/4 cup all-purpose flour

3 garlic cloves, pressed
3 tablespoons freshly grated asiago cheese
3 tablespoons chopped fresh mint leaves
1 teaspoon freshly ground pepper
1/4 teaspoon freshly grated nutmeg
Canola oil for frying
Salt and pepper to taste

EQUIPMENT NEEDED: A colander; a large skillet; a wire rack

Place the tomatoes in a colander and set aside to drain. Combine the zucchini and leeks in a medium bowl. Sprinkle with 1 1/2 teaspoons salt and let stand for 15 minutes; drain. Squeeze out any excess liquid. Stir in the eggs, flour, garlic, cheese, mint, pepper and nutmeg.

Heat a large skillet over medium-high heat. Pour 1/4 inch of oil into the skillet. Heat until the oil smokes. Drop the zucchini mixture carefully by 1/4 cupfuls into the hot oil. Fry until brown and crispy on each side, changing the oil between batches as necessary. Remove to a wire rack to cool.

Place the drained tomatoes in a bowl and sprinkle with salt and pepper to taste. Serve on top of the pancakes.

Note: A perfect dish to prepare in the heat of summer when the zucchini is abundant and only the best local tomatoes have ripened on their vines. Do not drain the pancakes on paper towels or the pancakes will become soggy.

Baked Stuffed Tomatoes

4 fresh tomatoes, rinsed and dried,
stems removed
3 slices bacon, cooked, drained and crumbled
1 tablespoon unsalted butter
1 tablespoon olive oil
1 small onion, chopped
2 garlic cloves, minced
1 ciabatta roll, cut into cubes
2 tablespoons mayonnaise

2 large basil leaves, chiffonade cut
Leaves from 2 sprigs of fresh oregano, chopped
Leaves from 2 sprigs of fresh thyme, chopped
1/4 cup (1 ounce) freshly grated
Parmesan cheese
Sea salt and freshly ground pepper to taste
Freshly grated Parmesan cheese for sprinkling
(optional)

EQUIPMENT NEEDED: A 9-inch baking dish; a medium skillet

Cut the tops off the tomatoes. Scoop out the centers of the tomatoes and place in a small bowl, reserving the shells. Chop the tops of the tomatoes and add to the tomato centers. Add the bacon and mix well. Arrange the reserved tomato shells in a 9-inch baking dish.

Melt the butter with the olive oil in a medium skillet over medium heat. Add the onion and garlic and sauté until light in color. Add to the tomato mixture. Stir in the ciabatta cubes, mayonnaise, basil, oregano, thyme, 1/4 cup Parmesan cheese, the salt and pepper.

Preheat the oven to 325 degrees. Lightly stuff the mixture into the tomato shells and sprinkle with additional Parmesan cheese. Bake for 25 minutes or until the tops are light brown. Let stand for 10 minutes before serving.

Note: This dish can be assembled in advance and heated before serving.

Companion Planting for Better Tomatoes

Planting chamomile near tomatoes encourages a large harvest. Garlic chives near tomatoes discourage rabbits and squirrels. Basil makes tomatoes taste better and attracts bees to aid pollination. Lemon balm and borage attract beneficial insects, but members of the *Brassica* family attract pests that attack tomatoes. Nasturtiums will help reduce fungal growth. Do not plant tomatoes near a black walnut tree. It will inhibit the tomato's growth.

Succotash

5 ears of corn
2 tablespoons olive oil
1/2 cup chopped yellow onion
1 garlic clove, chopped
1/4 cup (1/2 stick) unsalted butter
1 cup chopped red bell pepper
1 cup fresh or frozen okra

2 cups cooked baby lima beans
1/3 cup chicken stock (preferably homemade)
1 tablespoon chopped fresh basil leaves
1 teaspoon herbes de Provence
  (recipe follows)
Coarse salt and freshly ground pepper to taste

EQUIPMENT NEEDED: A large skillet; a medium baking dish

Remove the husks and silks from the corn. Using a sharp knife, cut the kernels into a bowl. Heat the olive oil in a large skillet over medium heat. Add the onion and garlic and sauté until light in color. Add the butter, corn, bell pepper and okra. Cook until the vegetables are tender. Stir in the lima beans, stock, basil, herbes de Provence, salt and pepper. Cook until heated through. Remove from the heat. Let stand for 10 minutes so the flavors can meld before serving.

Note: Succotash is a true American dish, and every region has its own version. Originally a Native American Narraganset dish, it was simply boiled corn.

Herbes de Provence

1/4 cup dried chives
1/4 cup dried oregano
1/4 cup dried rosemary
2 tablespoons dried basil

1 teaspoon celery seeds
1 teaspoon fennel seeds
1/2 teaspoon dried lavender flowers

EQUIPMENT NEEDED: An airtight container

Combine the chives, oregano, rosemary, basil, celery seeds, fennel seeds and lavender flowers in a bowl and mix well. Store in an airtight container.

Dill and Fennel Seeds

During the early years of the American colonies, when Puritan church services might last all day, worshipers often took dill or fennel seeds to chew on to prevent sleepiness. Hence, these seeds became known as "meeting seeds." Chewing dill or fennel seeds will often tame an upset stomach and are offered in many parts of India as a digestive aid and breath freshener after meals.

Balsamic-Glazed Harvest Vegetables

2 cups balsamic vinegar

6 to 8 large garlic cloves

12 red, white or yellow new potatoes, scrubbed
    and cut into 1-inch pieces

1 beet, cut into 1/2-inch wedges

2 carrots, peeled and cut into 1-inch pieces

2 parsnips, peeled and cut into 1-inch pieces

1 turnip, peeled and cut into 1/2-inch wedges

1 red or white onion, cut into 1/2-inch wedges

1 sweet potato, peeled and cut into 1-inch pieces

1 fennel bulb, cut into 1/2-inch wedges

1 red, orange or yellow bell pepper, cut into
    1/2-inch wedges

1 cup broccoli florets, cut into 1/2-inch pieces

2 tablespoons butter, melted

3 tablespoons olive oil

1 tablespoon fresh thyme, minced

1 tablespoon fresh rosemary, minced

Coarse salt and freshly ground pepper to taste

Chopped fresh flat-leaf parsley for garnish

EQUIPMENT NEEDED: A medium saucepan; a 10×15-inch baking pan

Bring the balsamic vinegar to a boil in a medium saucepan. Boil until thick and syrupy and reduced by half, watching carefully to prevent burning.

Preheat the oven to 425 degrees. Place the garlic and vegetables in a large sealable plastic bag. Add the butter, olive oil, thyme, rosemary, salt and pepper. Seal the bag and shake until the vegetables are coated. Place the garlic, new potatoes, beet, carrots, parsnips and turnip in a greased 10×15-inch baking pan. Bake for 10 minutes. Add the onion, sweet potato and fennel. Bake for 10 minutes longer. Add the bell pepper and broccoli. Bake for 10 minutes longer. Remove from the oven. Drizzle with the reduced balsamic vinegar and toss to coat. Bake for 4 minutes. Sprinkle with salt and pepper. Garnish with parsley. Serve hot or at room temperature.

Note: This dish is well worth a trip to the farmers' market for the very best seasonal vegetables. Be creative with other seasonal vegetables such as parsley root, butternut squash, cauliflower, celery root, endive, asparagus, and green beans.

 ## Onions

All varieties of onion will induce tearing when you cut them. They release a volatile gas that contains a dilution of sulphuric acid, which is an eye irritant. To minimize this effect, cut off the root end of the onion and discard. The root end has more enzymes that initiate the process of sulphuric acid formation.

Roasted Root Vegetable Mash with Truffle Oil

SERVES 8 TO 10

4 sprigs of fresh rosemary
8 sprigs of fresh thyme
4 carrots, peeled and chopped
4 parsnips, peeled and coarsely chopped
1 large sweet potato, peeled and
    coarsely chopped
1 rutabaga, peeled and coarsely chopped
4 garlic cloves

Coarse salt and freshly ground pepper to taste
Extra-virgin olive oil for drizzling
4 large Idaho potatoes, peeled and
    coarsely chopped
$1/2$ cup (1 stick) unsalted butter, cut into cubes
2 to $2^1/2$ cups half-and-half, warmed
Truffle oil for drizzling

EQUIPMENT NEEDED: A 10×15-inch baking pan; a large saucepan; a potato masher or electric hand mixer

Preheat the oven to 400 degrees. Lay the rosemary and thyme in a 10×15-inch baking dish. Combine the carrots, parsnips, sweet potato, rutabaga and garlic in a medium bowl. Sprinkle liberally with salt and pepper. Drizzle with enough olive oil to coat lightly and toss to mix. Spread the vegetables over the herbs. Roast, uncovered, for 40 to 50 minutes or until the vegetables are soft.

Place the Idaho potatoes in a large saucepan and cover with salted cold water. Bring to a boil; reduce the heat to medium. Cook, partially covered, for 20 minutes or until tender. Drain the potatoes thoroughly and return to the saucepan. Add the roasted vegetables, discarding the herbs. Add the butter and 2 cups of the half-and-half. Mash with a potato masher or beat with an electric mixer until smooth but slightly chunky. Add the remaining half-and-half if needed for the desired consistency. Sprinkle with salt and pepper. Keep warm in a 250-degree oven until ready to serve. Drizzle with truffle oil at serving time.

Note: This colorful and hearty dish is wonderful in the fall when the weather gets cold and your appetite comes alive.

Meats

Beef Tenderloin with Cognac Mustard Sauce

6 (4-ounce) beef tenderloin fillets
1 tablespoon unsalted butter
4 shallots, minced
2 cups beef stock (preferably homemade)
2 tablespoons Cognac
2 tablespoons Dijon mustard
3 tablespoons finely chopped fresh flat-leaf parsley
1/2 cup (1 stick) unsalted butter, cut into 8 pieces
Salt and freshly ground pepper to taste

EQUIPMENT NEEDED: An outdoor grill; a medium saucepan

Preheat an outdoor grill. Place the fillets on the grill rack. Grill to 145 degrees on a meat thermometer for medium-rare or to the desired degree of doneness. Place on a warm platter and cover loosely to keep warm.

Melt 1 tablespoon butter in a medium saucepan over medium heat. Add the shallots. Sauté for 2 minutes or until soft. Add the stock. Bring to a boil and cook until the mixture is reduced by one-half. Add the Cognac and boil for 1 minute. Reduce the heat to low. Whisk in the Dijon mustard and parsley. Stir in 1/2 cup butter one piece at a time. Sprinkle with salt and pepper. Pour over the fillets and serve.

Note: The best cut of beef deserves the best sauce.

 ## Shallots
Milder and sweeter than onions with a hint of garlic, shallots grow in small bulb clusters and have a copper-colored skin. Just like onions and garlic, shallots should be sautéed only to transparency, or they will impart a bitter flavor to food. If a shallot is not available, use a scallion rubbed with the cut side of a garlic clove.

Peppered Roast Beef Tenderloin with Garlic Oregano Sauce

BEEF TENDERLOIN
4 pounds beef tenderloin, eye-of-round roast
   or boneless rump roast
4 to 6 garlic cloves, sliced
1/4 cup olive oil
1 tablespoon coarse salt
1 tablespoon freshly ground pepper
1/2 teaspoon each dried oregano, dried
   rosemary and dried thyme

GARLIC OREGANO SAUCE
1/2 cup mayonnaise
1/2 cup sour cream
1 garlic clove, minced
1 tablespoon chopped fresh oregano
2 tablespoons prepared horseradish
1 tablespoon fresh lemon juice
1/2 teaspoon coarse salt

EQUIPMENT NEEDED: A roasting pan with wire rack

To prepare the tenderloin, preheat the oven to 500 degrees. Make small incisions in the tenderloin with a sharp paring knife and insert the garlic. Rub with the olive oil. Mix the salt, pepper, oregano, rosemary and thyme in a bowl and rub over the surface of the tenderloin. Place on a rack in a roasting pan. Roast for 15 minutes. Reduce the heat to 300 degrees. Roast for 30 to 45 minutes longer or to 145 degrees on a meat thermometer for medium-rare. Let stand for 10 to 15 minutes before slicing.

To prepare the sauce, combine the mayonnaise, sour cream, garlic, oregano, horseradish, lemon juice and salt in a small bowl and mix well. Serve with the tenderloin.

Note: This roast beef is a perfect example of how to successfully combine the use of fresh and dried herbs.

Herbed Grilled Steak with Blue Cheese

2 teaspoons coarse salt
2 garlic cloves, crushed
2 teaspoons chopped fresh garlic chives
2 teaspoons chopped fresh oregano
2 teaspoons chopped fresh flat-leaf parsley
2 teaspoons chopped fresh summer savory

1 teaspoon coarsely cracked pepper
2 teaspoons (or more) extra-virgin olive oil
2 (1 1/2-inch) beef steaks such as sirloin, rib-eye
   or T-bone
2 tablespoons crumbled good-quality
   blue cheese

EQUIPMENT NEEDED: A mortar with a pestle; an outdoor grill

Mash the salt with the garlic in a mortar with a pestle. Add the garlic chives, oregano, parsley, savory and pepper, mashing and stirring after each addition until well mixed. Stir in enough olive oil to form a smooth paste. Preheat an outdoor grill. Coat both sides of the steaks with the herb paste and place on the grill rack. Grill for 5 minutes on each side or to 145 degrees on a meat thermometer for medium-rare, turning once. Remove the steaks to a warm plate with the hottest side up. Sprinkle with the blue cheese and serve.

Note: Garlic chives have long, thin, flat stems with a flavor more like garlic than chives, though milder. Both the leaves and stems are used. If making paste for several steaks, a food processor can be used to chop herbs, but do not overprocess. The flavor comes from the pronounced texture of the herbs.

Flank Steak with Roquefort Butter

SERVES 4

1 (1 1/2-pound) flank steak, scored to prevent
    edges from curling
2 tablespoons red wine vinegar
6 tablespoons olive oil
Salt and freshly ground pepper to taste

1/4 cup (1/2 stick) butter, softened
1/2 cup crumbled Roquefort cheese
1 garlic clove, minced
1 tablespoon chopped fresh chives
2 tablespoons brandy

EQUIPMENT NEEDED: A shallow glass dish; an outdoor grill

Place the flank steak in a shallow glass dish. Whisk the vinegar, olive oil, salt and pepper in a bowl. Pour over the steak. Marinate, covered, in the refrigerator for 2 hours or longer, turning several times. Preheat an outdoor grill to high. Drain the steak, discarding the marinade. Place the steak on the grill rack. Grill over hot coals for 4 minutes on each side or to 145 degrees on a meat thermometer for medium-rare. Place on a warm serving plate and let stand for 10 minutes. Mix the butter and cheese in a bowl until smooth. Add the garlic, chives and brandy and mix well. Cut the steak thinly across the grain. Spoon the butter over the steak and serve.

Steak with Cream of Juniper Sauce

SERVES 4

1 (1 1/4-pound) beef sirloin steak (see Note)
Coarse salt and freshly ground pepper to taste
2 tablespoons olive oil
1 tablespoon unsalted butter
2 shallots, minced
1 tablespoon juniper berries, crushed
1/4 cup gin

1 cup veal stock or beef stock
    (preferably homemade)
1/2 cup heavy cream
1 tablespoon chopped fresh rosemary
1 tablespoon chopped fresh thyme
Chopped flat-leaf parsley for garnish

EQUIPMENT NEEDED: A medium skillet

Sprinkle the steak with salt and pepper. Heat the olive oil in a medium skillet over medium-high heat. Add the steak. Cook for 3 minutes on each side or until brown but still pink inside. Remove to a warm dish and cover with foil. Reduce the heat to medium. Melt the butter in the pan drippings in the skillet. Add the shallots and juniper berries. Sauté for 1 minute or until soft. Add the gin and stock, stirring to deglaze the skillet by scraping the bottom to dislodge any browned bits. Cook for 5 minutes or until the stock is reduced slightly. Stir in the cream. Cook for 5 minutes or until the sauce is reduced. Add the rosemary, thyme, salt and pepper. Cut the steak against the grain and spoon the sauce over the top. Garnish with parsley.

Note: Astringent juniper berries are crushed to release their essence into this rich dish. Four 4-ounce beef tenderloin fillets may be used instead of the sirloin. Serve the fillets whole with the sauce.

 ## Juniper

Juniper berries are best known as the primary flavoring in gin, but they have many culinary uses. Particularly popular in Northern Europe where they are used in marinades, sauces, sauerkrauts, and sausages, the berries are best when crushed, or bruised, before using. They have a strong, piney, cleansing aroma reminiscent of the outdoors, so they are perfect for cutting rich, fatty game meats such as venison, rabbit, goose, duck, and wild boar.

Chimichurri Flank Steak Roulade

2/3 cup sherry vinegar
1/2 cup chopped fresh flat-leaf parsley
3 tablespoons chopped fresh oregano
2 tablespoons fresh lemon juice
5 large garlic cloves, minced

3 tablespoons extra-virgin olive oil
1 (11/2- to 2-pound) flank steak, pounded to 1/2-inch thickness, or butterflied or cubed by butcher
2 tablespoons extra-virgin olive oil

EQUIPMENT NEEDED: A large ovenproof skillet with a lid

Preheat the oven to 325 degrees. Whisk the vinegar, parsley, oregano, lemon juice and garlic in a bowl. Add 3 tablespoons olive oil gradually, whisking constantly. Spread over the flank steak, leaving a 1-inch border on each side. Roll up and secure with kitchen twine every 3 inches, or secure with wooden picks or skewers. Brown on all sides in 2 tablespoons olive oil in a large ovenproof skillet over medium-high heat. Bake, covered, for 1 hour or to 145 degrees on a meat thermometer. Let stand for 10 minutes. Remove the twine and cut the steak into slices.

Note: Chimichurri, a corruption of the name "Jimmy McCurry," is a thick herb sauce as common to Argentines as steak sauce is to Americans. The flank steak should be thin enough to roll easily when stuffed with South America's version of pesto.

Bay Leaf-Braised Short Ribs

8 beef short ribs
Salt and freshly ground pepper to taste
3 tablespoons olive oil
1 onion, chopped
1 carrot, peeled and chopped
1 rib celery, chopped
1 parsnip, peeled and chopped

1 fennel bulb, sliced
4 ounces pancetta, chopped
6 garlic cloves, minced
1 bottle full-bodied red wine
8 bay leaves
2 cups chopped seeded peeled tomatoes
1/4 cup chopped fresh tarragon for garnish

EQUIPMENT NEEDED: A Dutch oven

Sprinkle the ribs with salt and pepper. Heat the olive oil in a Dutch oven. Add the ribs and cook until brown on all sides. Remove the ribs and set aside. Drain any excess oil from the Dutch oven. Add the onion, carrot, celery, parsnip, fennel and pancetta to the Dutch oven. Sauté for 10 minutes. Add the garlic and sauté for 1 minute. Add the wine and bring to a boil. Add the bay leaves and tomatoes. Return the ribs to the Dutch oven. Bring to a boil; reduce the heat. Simmer, covered, for 3 to 4 hours or until the ribs are very tender. Let stand to cool. Chill, covered, for 8 to 10 hours. Skim the surface to remove the excess fat. Discard the bay leaves. Reheat and garnish with the tarragon.

Note: Plan ahead to make these delicious short ribs.

Apple Cheeseburgers with Lemon Horseradish Mousse

1¹/2 pounds ground chuck
1 cup (4 ounces) coarsely shredded
   Cheddar cheese
1 apple, peeled and finely chopped
2 egg yolks

Coarse salt and freshly ground pepper to taste
1 tablespoon unsalted butter
2 tablespoons vegetable oil
4 hamburger buns, split and toasted
Lemon Horseradish Mousse (recipe follows)

EQUIPMENT NEEDED: A large skillet or outdoor grill

Pat the ground chuck into a rectangle on a work surface. Sprinkle with the cheese and apple. Add the egg yolks, salt and pepper. Fold the ground chuck over the top and mix lightly. Shape into four patties. Melt the butter with the oil in a large skillet over medium-high heat or preheat an outdoor grill. Add the patties and cook to 160 degrees on a meat thermometer. Place on the bottom half of the buns and top with the mousse. Replace the top halves of the buns and serve.

Note: With every bite of this unique burger, the creamy mousse will melt down into every crevice.

Lemon Horseradish Mousse

2 cups sour cream
1 cup drained prepared horseradish
2 envelopes unflavored gelatin
1 cup hot water

¹/4 cup sugar
Juice and zest of 1 lemon
2 tablespoons tarragon vinegar
¹/2 teaspoon salt

EQUIPMENT NEEDED: A 4-cup decorative mold

Mix the sour cream and horseradish in a bowl. Soften the gelatin in a small amount of cold water. Dissolve the softened gelatin in the hot water in a bowl. Stir in the sugar, lemon juice, lemon zest, vinegar and salt. Add the sour cream mixture and mix well. Pour into a 4-cup decorative mold. Chill for 1 hour or until set. Unmold and serve.

Note: Wonderful with beef in any form, this mousse is also good with ham. Try the leftovers on sandwiches in place of mayonnaise.

Veal Ragoût with Red Wine in Puff Pastry

1/4 cup extra-virgin olive oil
2 pounds veal shoulder, cut into 1-inch pieces
4 ounces thick-cut bacon, cut into 1/4-inch
   pieces (about 4 slices)
1 small red onion, chopped into 1/4-inch pieces
   (about 1 cup)
2 carrots, chopped into 1/4-inch pieces
   (about 1 cup)
1 rib celery, chopped into 1/4-inch pieces
   (about 1/3 cup)
4 ounces fresh mushrooms, chopped

2 tablespoons paprika
1 teaspoon dried marjoram
1 teaspoon dried rosemary
1/4 teaspoon cinnamon
1 cup red wine
1 cup veal stock or rich chicken stock
   (preferably homemade)
Coarse salt and freshly ground pepper to taste
1 (17-ounce) package frozen puff pastry, thawed
Egg wash for brushing

EQUIPMENT NEEDED: A medium Dutch oven; a rolling pin; a baking sheet; a silicone baking pad or baking parchment

Heat the olive oil in a medium Dutch oven over medium-high heat. Cook the veal in batches in the hot olive oil until golden brown. Remove the veal to a bowl and set aside. Add the bacon, onion, carrots and celery to the pan drippings in the Dutch oven. Cook for 5 minutes or until softened. Add the mushrooms and cook until softened. Stir in the paprika, marjoram, rosemary and cinnamon. Cook for 1 minute. Add the wine and stock and bring to a boil. Add the veal with accumulated juices and return to a boil. Reduce the heat. Simmer, covered, for 1 1/2 hours or until the veal is tender. Let stand until cool. Sprinkle with salt and pepper. Chill, covered, for 4 to 10 hours.

Preheat the oven to 400 degrees. Roll one sheet of the puff pastry into a 12×14-inch rectangle on a work surface. Spread one-half of the cold ragoût over the pastry, leaving a 1-inch border. Roll up from the long side and pinch the edges to seal. Place on a baking sheet lined with a silicone baking pad or baking parchment. (A silicone baking pad is recommended to prevent the pastry from tearing.) Repeat with the remaining pastry and ragoût. Brush each with egg wash. Cut three vents in the top of each to allow steam to escape. Bake for 20 to 30 minutes or until the pastry is golden brown. Cut each pastry into three or four diagonal slices and serve.

Note: Fun to make, this beautiful dish makes a dramatic presentation.

 ## Sweet Marjoram
Sweet marjoram is one of the great culinary herbs, having a more delicate flavor than its cousin, oregano. Its soft, pervasive flavor is suited to many dishes. Combined with other herbs, it serves as a catalyst, balancing all. As such, marjoram is often called "the marrying herb," as it softens the flavors produced when several herbs are used in a single recipe so that none overpowers another.

Herb-Encrusted Rack of Lamb

1 (8-rib) Frenched rack of lamb
1/2 garlic clove, minced
1/2 teaspoon chopped fresh thyme
Coarse salt and freshly ground pepper to taste
2 tablespoons (or more) olive oil
2 or 3 garlic cloves, minced
Zest of 1 lemon

Juice of 1/2 large lemon
1 tablespoon finely chopped fresh mint leaves
1 teaspoon chopped fresh thyme or
   lemon thyme
1 teaspoon finely chopped fresh rosemary
1 tablespoon Dijon mustard
1 cup fresh bread crumbs

EQUIPMENT NEEDED: A medium skillet; an outdoor charcoal grill

Rub the entire surface of the lamb with 1/2 clove garlic, 1/2 teaspoon thyme, salt and pepper. Heat the olive oil in a medium skillet over medium heat. Add 2 or 3 garlic cloves. Cook for 1 minute or until the oil is fragrant, being careful to not brown the garlic or it will become bitter. Remove the skillet from the heat. Stir in the lemon zest, lemon juice, mint, 1 teaspoon thyme, the rosemary and Dijon mustard. Add the bread crumbs and mix well, adding olive oil if needed to make a moist but not wet crumb coating. Pat both sides of the lamb with the coating.

Preheat an outdoor charcoal grill to medium. Rub the grill rack with oil. Place the lamb meat side down on the prepared rack, turning carefully so the coating remains on the lamb. Grill to 145 degrees on a meat thermometer for medium-rare. Remove to a carving board. Let stand for 10 to 15 minutes before carving into individual chops.

Note: We prefer our rack of lamb grilled over charcoal, but it is also good roasted in a 425-degree oven for 20 minutes or to 145 degrees on a meat thermometer.

 ## Mints

There are over forty varieties of *Mentha*, or mint. The most popular are spearmint, peppermint, and pennyroyal. Spearmint is preferred for most culinary dishes, such as grilled meats and stuffed vegetables. Peppermint is a favorite in dessert dishes and is also cultivated for its oil. Pennyroyal is used to season haggis and black puddings. Mint is extremely invasive and best grown in a flowerpot.

Mint (*Mentha* spp.)

Pork Tenderloin with Nine-Herb Green Sauce SERVES 4 TO 6

PORK
1 (1½- to 2-pound) pork tenderloin,
    silver skin removed
Olive oil for rubbing
Coarse salt and freshly ground pepper to taste

NINE-HERB GREEN SAUCE
2 hard-cooked eggs
3 tablespoons vegetable oil
⅔ cup yogurt
⅔ cup sour cream

1 shallot, minced
1 garlic clove, pressed
1 cornichon (gherkin pickle), minced
Juice of ½ lemon
1 teaspoon German-style prepared mustard
A pinch of sugar
Choice of 9 fresh herbs, such as borage,
    chervil, chives, dandelion leaves, dill,
    lemon balm, lovage, parsley, salad burnet,
    sorrel, spinach, tarragon and/or watercress
Salt and freshly ground pepper taste

EQUIPMENT NEEDED: An outdoor grill

To prepare the pork, preheat an outdoor grill. Rub the pork with olive oil and sprinkle with salt and pepper. Place on the grill rack. Grill to 160 degrees on a meat thermometer. Place on a warm platter and cover loosely with foil. Let stand for 10 minutes.

To prepare the sauce, cut the eggs into halves. Place the egg yolks in a small bowl and mash until smooth, reserving the egg whites. Add the oil and mix to form a smooth paste. Stir in the yogurt and sour cream. Add the shallot, garlic, pickle, lemon juice, mustard and sugar. Chop nine herbs of choice to taste. Add to the sauce. Mince the egg whites. Add to the sauce and mix well. Season with salt and pepper.

To serve, carve the pork into slices and serve with the sauce.

Note: Make this green sauce when your herb garden is at its peak. Choose nine herbs and use as much or as little of them as you like. The sauce is also good served with beef, boiled potatoes, or omelets.

 Borage
Borage was grown in the gardens of King Louis IV of France. Europeans brought it to America to flavor their claret. Borage has one of the few truly blue-colored, edible flowers. With a honey-like taste, the flowers are often used to decorate desserts. Candied borage flowers are made by dipping the flowers in hot sugar syrup and then tossing in ice.

Globe amaranth (*Gomphrena globosa*)

Herb Butter Pork Rib Roast

3 tablespoons butter, softened
2 tablespoons minced shallots
2 garlic cloves, minced
1 teaspoon Dijon mustard

2 tablespoons chopped fresh flat-leaf parsley
1 tablespoon chopped fresh tarragon
1 (4-rib) rack of pork
Salt and freshly ground pepper to taste

EQUIPMENT NEEDED: A roasting pan with a rack

Preheat the oven to 400 degrees. Combine the butter, shallots, garlic, Dijon mustard, parsley and tarragon in a bowl and mix to form a paste. Sprinkle the pork with salt and pepper. Place on a rack in a roasting pan. Spread the herb butter on top of the pork. Roast for 15 minutes. Reduce the oven temperature to 300 degrees. Roast for 1 1/2 hours longer or to 160 degrees on a meat thermometer. Remove from the oven and let stand for 15 minutes before carving.

Note: This simple roast slow cooks and fills the kitchen with the sweet smell of herbs.

Pork Chops with Anjou Pears and Lemon Sauce

SERVES 2

2 tablespoons olive oil
2 (4-ounce) boneless center-cut pork
   loin chops (about 3/4 inch thick)
1/4 teaspoon salt
1/4 teaspoon cracked pepper
2 tablespoons olive oil
2 Anjou pears (about 1 pound), peeled and
   cut into halves

1/4 cup dry white wine
2 teaspoons grated lemon zest
1 tablespoon fresh lemon juice
1 tablespoon chopped fresh lemon thyme
1 tablespoon chopped fresh chives
1/4 teaspoon salt
1/4 teaspoon cracked pepper

EQUIPMENT NEEDED: A large skillet

Heat 2 tablespoons olive oil in a large skillet over medium-high heat. Sprinkle the pork with 1/4 teaspoon salt and 1/4 teaspoon pepper. Cook the pork in the hot olive oil for 3 minutes on each side or to 160 degrees on a meat thermometer. Remove the pork from the skillet and keep warm.

Heat 2 tablespoons olive oil with the drippings in the skillet over medium-high heat. Add the pears cut side down. Cook for 2 minutes on each side or until golden brown. Remove from the skillet and keep warm. Add the wine to the drippings in the skillet, stirring to deglaze by scraping the bottom of the skillet to loosen the browned bits. Stir in the lemon zest, lemon juice, lemon thyme, chives, 1/4 teaspoon salt and 1/4 teaspoon pepper. Cook for 1 minute. Serve the pork with the pears and sauce.

Note: Lemon three ways breathes new life into this traditional pork and pear dish and warms a cool autumn evening. Anjou pears are at their peak in the fall.

Cassoulet

1 cup dried Great Northern beans
2 slices bacon, chopped
2 leeks, white and pale green parts thinly sliced
1 rib celery, sliced
8 ounces sausage, such as andouille or
   Italian sausage, chopped
3 garlic cloves, minced

1 tablespoon olive oil
Salt and freshly ground pepper to taste
1/4 cup brandy
1 cup chopped tomatoes
2 cups chicken stock (preferably homemade)
1 tablespoon sugar (optional)
2 tablespoons chopped fresh sage leaves

EQUIPMENT NEEDED: A medium saucepan; a medium heavy stockpot, Dutch oven or ovenproof stockpot

Sort and rinse the beans. Soak the beans in water to cover in a bowl for 8 to 10 hours. Drain the beans, discarding the liquid. Place in a medium saucepan and cover with water. Bring to a boil. Reduce the heat and simmer for 1 hour or until tender.

Sauté the bacon, leeks and celery in a medium heavy stockpot or Dutch oven for a few minutes. Add the sausage, garlic and olive oil. Season well with salt and pepper. Cook until the leeks are golden brown. Add the brandy, stirring to deglaze the stockpot by scraping the bottom to loosen up the browned bits. Add the tomatoes, stock, sugar and sage. Drain the beans, discarding the liquid. Stir into the sausage mixture. Bring to a boil. Reduce the heat and simmer for 1 hour.

Note: For an impressive rustic presentation, cook and serve the cassoulet in an enameled Dutch oven. The cassoulet may be baked in a Dutch oven or ovenproof stockpot in a 325-degree oven for 1 hour.

Chinese Five-Spice Powder

The name comes not from the number of spices in the powder, but rather from the number of flavors: sweet, sour, bitter, pungent, and salty. To prepare, toast the seeds from 10 cardamom pods, 2 (3-inch) cinnamon sticks, 4 teaspoons whole peppercorns, 1 tablespoon whole cloves, 1 tablespoon fennel seeds and 2 teaspoons star anise seeds separately on a baking sheet in a 350-degree oven until aromatic. Process all of the toasted spices together in a small food processor or a coffee grinder until ground to a fine powder. Store in an airtight container.

Poultry & Seafood

Salmon Poached in Lobster Bisque with Thai Seasonings, page 138

Roast Chicken with Figs and Apricots

1 cup chopped yellow onion
4 large garlic cloves, chopped
1 cup chicken stock (preferably homemade)
1/4 cup fresh orange juice
1 teaspoon ground coriander
1/2 teaspoon cinnamon
1/2 teaspoon ground cumin
1/4 teaspoon ground cloves
1/2 teaspoon salt
Freshly ground pepper to taste
1 (4-pound) chicken, cut into serving pieces
1 cup dried figs, pitted dates or pitted prunes
1 cup dried pitted apricots
1/2 cup slivered almonds
Hot cooked couscous

EQUIPMENT NEEDED: A 9×13-inch glass baking dish

Mix the onion, garlic, stock, orange juice, coriander, cinnamon, cumin, cloves, salt and pepper in a medium bowl. Place the chicken in a large sealable plastic bag. Add the marinade and seal the bag. Marinate in the refrigerator for 8 to 10 hours, turning several times.

Preheat the oven to 350 degrees. Place the chicken in a 9×13-inch glass baking dish and pour the marinade over the top. Bake, uncovered, for 1 hour, basting with the marinade several times. Add the figs and apricots. Bake, covered, for 30 minutes or until the chicken is cooked through. Remove from the oven and let stand for 10 minutes. Uncover the chicken and sprinkle with the almonds. Serve with couscous, spooning some of the sauce over the couscous.

Note: Aromatic spices and sweet fruits give this roast chicken served with couscous a Middle Eastern flair.

Chicken en Papillote with Lemon

1/3 cup chopped fresh dill
1/3 cup chopped fresh mint leaves
1/3 cup chopped fresh flat-leaf parsley
2 garlic cloves, minced
Salt and freshly ground pepper to taste
6 boneless skinless chicken breasts
6 tablespoons butter
2 lemons, sliced

EQUIPMENT NEEDED: Baking parchment; a large baking sheet

Preheat the oven to 400 degrees. Mix the dill, mint, parsley, garlic, salt and pepper in a small bowl. Cut six 14-inch hearts out of baking parchment. Place a chicken breast on one side of each heart and sprinkle with salt and pepper. Sprinkle each with about 2 tablespoons of the herb mixture. Dot with 1 tablespoon of the butter and top with 2 lemon slices. Fold the remaining half of the heart over the chicken and fold the edges together to seal, beginning at the top of the heart in the center of the dip and continuing in small increments until reaching the end of the heart. Tuck the last fold under to form a tightly sealed packet. Place the packets on a large baking sheet. Bake for 15 minutes or until the chicken is cooked through. Serve immediately.

Note: The technique "en papillote," or "in parchment," is used to steam food in the oven in its own juices. The result is dramatic. Serve on plates and allow guests to slice open the packets, releasing the aromas. Provide good bread to sop up the juices.

Mahimahi Tacos with Avocado Mango Salsa SERVES 6

AVOCADO MANGO SALSA
3 mangoes, finely chopped
1 avocado, finely chopped
1/2 red onion, minced
2 jalapeño chiles, seeded and minced
1 bunch cilantro, chopped
2 tablespoons fresh lime juice
2 tablespoons fresh orange juice
Salt and freshly ground pepper to taste

TACOS
Vegetable oil for frying
6 large white corn tortillas
6 (4-ounce) mahimahi fillets
Extra-virgin olive oil for brushing
Salt and pepper to taste
1 cup sour cream

EQUIPMENT NEEDED: A large cast-iron skillet

To prepare the salsa, combine the mangoes, avocado, onion, jalapeño chiles, cilantro, lime juice, orange juice, salt and pepper in a medium bowl and mix well.

To prepare the tacos, heat 1 tablespoon vegetable oil in a large cast-iron skillet. Fry the tortillas in batches in the hot oil until crisp on both sides, adding vegetable oil as needed. Fold the tortillas to form a shell. Remove to a plate and cover to keep warm. Wipe out the skillet and increase the heat to high. Brush the fish with olive oil and sprinkle with salt and pepper. Place in the hot skillet. Cook for 5 minutes per side or until the fish flakes easily. Remove to a cutting board. Cut the fish into 1 1/2- to 2-inch pieces. Spoon into the tortilla shells and top with the salsa and sour cream.

Note: A delightful change from traditional tacos, ours are refreshingly light. You can also grill the mahimahi fillets, if desired.

Poultry & Seafood

Pot marigold (*Calendula officinalis*)

Trout Steaks with Herbed Crust and Dill Sauce

SERVES 6

DILL SAUCE
1 cup Greek yogurt
3 tablespoons dill pickle juice
1/4 cup freshly chopped dill
1/4 cup freshly chopped garlic chives
1/8 teaspoon salt

FISH
1 (3- to 4-pound) trout, head and tail removed
1/4 cup olive oil
2 cups dry bread crumbs
1/4 cup olive oil
1/2 cup tarragon white wine vinegar or basil white wine vinegar
1 tablespoon Worcestershire sauce
2 teaspoons prepared mustard
Juice of 1 lime
1/4 teaspoon chopped fresh chervil
1/4 teaspoon chopped fresh lovage
1/4 teaspoon chopped fresh savory
1/4 teaspoon cayenne pepper
1/8 teaspoon coarse salt
1/8 teaspoon white pepper
2 teaspoons paprika

EQUIPMENT NEEDED: An 11×14-inch baking dish

To prepare the sauce, combine the yogurt, pickle juice, dill, garlic chives and salt in a bowl and mix well. Chill, covered, for 4 hours or up to 1 week before serving.

To prepare the fish, preheat the oven to 350 degrees. Cut the fish into six steaks. Pour 1/4 cup olive oil evenly into an 11×14-inch baking dish. Cover with the bread crumbs. Arrange the fish on top with the sides touching but not overlapping. Mix 1/4 cup olive oil, the vinegar, Worcestershire sauce, mustard, lime juice, chervil, lovage, savory, cayenne pepper, salt and white pepper in a bowl. Pour over the fish. Bake, uncovered, on the center oven rack for 15 minutes. Remove from the oven and sprinkle with the paprika. Return to the oven and bake for 5 minutes or until the fish flakes easily with a fork. Spoon the herbed crust over the hot fish and serve with the sauce on the side.

Dwarf pomegranate (*Punica granatum*)

Crab Dumplings with Bird's-Eye Chile Dipping Sauce

DUMPLINGS
1 pound crab meat, shells removed and
   meat flaked
1/2 cup fresh cilantro, chopped
Chiffonade of 2 shiso leaves (Japanese basil)
1 garlic clove, minced
1 tablespoon thinly sliced scallions
1 tablespoon minced jalapeño chile
1 teaspoon minced fresh gingerroot
1 tablespoon hoisin sauce
1 teaspoon soy sauce
1 teaspoon sesame oil
2 eggs, beaten

1 tablespoon all-purpose flour
1 cup panko (Japanese bread crumbs)
30 round won ton wrappers
1 banana leaf (see Note)

BIRD'S-EYE CHILE DIPPING SAUCE
1/2 cup fish sauce
1 tablespoon rice wine vinegar
1 teaspoon sugar
1 scallion, sliced
1 bird's-eye chile, sliced
1 shiso leaf, chiffonade cut (Japanese basil)

EQUIPMENT NEEDED: A bamboo or metal steamer

To prepare the dumplings, combine the crab meat, cilantro, shiso, garlic, scallions, jalapeño chile, gingerroot, hoisin sauce, soy sauce, sesame oil, eggs, flour and panko in a large bowl and stir to mix well. Place a spoonful of the crab meat mixture in the center of each won ton wrapper. Moisten the edge with water and fold over to enclose the filling, sealing the edge to form a dumpling. Set aside on a lightly floured surface until ready to steam. Line a bamboo or metal steamer with the banana leaf. Arrange a single layer of the dumplings on the banana leaf, making sure the dumplings do not touch. Steam, covered, for 15 to 20 minutes. Repeat in batches with the remaining dumplings until all have been steamed.

To prepare the sauce, combine the fish sauce, vinegar and sugar in a small bowl and stir until the sugar dissolves. Stir in the scallion, bird's-eye chile and shiso. Serve in small dipping bowls with the dumplings.

Note: The tiny bird's-eye chiles are the hottest of Thai peppers, often referred to as "peri-peri." For a slightly milder chile, try a cayenne or serrano. Banana leaves are available at international markets.

Banana
Surprisingly, the banana plant is actually an herb, which makes it the world's tallest herb. Its elongated fruit is not a true fruit but rather a false berry. As the banana skin turns from green to black, the interior changes from complex starch to simple sugar. Many consider blackened bananas best for cooking because of the intense sweetness. Banana leaves are waterproof and used effectively to wrap food for cooking or storage.

Poultry & Seafood

Rock Shrimp Cakes with Peach and Mint Aïoli

PEACH AND MINT AÏOLI
1/3 cup puréed peaches
1/2 cup mayonnaise
1 teaspoon sugar
1 teaspoon chopped mint leaves
1/2 teaspoon minced garlic
1/2 teaspoon grated fresh gingerroot
Zest and juice of 1 lemon
Coarse salt and freshly ground pepper to taste

ROCK SHRIMP CAKES
2 pounds rock shrimp or gulf shrimp, peeled, deveined and chopped

1/4 cup fresh lime juice
2 eggs
2 tablespoons chopped fresh chives
2 tablespoons chopped fresh cilantro
1 tablespoon crab seasoning blend
2 tablespoons Dijon mustard
1/3 cup panko (Japanese bread crumbs) plus more for sprinkling
Butter for frying

EQUIPMENT NEEDED: A large nonstick skillet; a large baking sheet

To prepare the aïoli, combine the peach purée, mayonnaise, sugar, mint, garlic, gingerroot, lemon zest and lemon juice in a small bowl and mix well. Sprinkle with salt and pepper. Chill, covered, until serving time.

To prepare the shrimp cakes, combine the shrimp, lime juice, eggs, chives, cilantro, crab seasoning blend and Dijon mustard in a large bowl and mix well. Stir in 1/3 cup of the panko. Chill, covered, for 1 hour. Preheat the oven to 350 degrees. Shape the shrimp mixture into sixteen patties. Lightly sprinkle the top and bottom of each with additional panko. Cook the patties in melted butter in a large nonstick skillet over medium heat for 1 minute per side or until light brown. Place on a large baking sheet. Bake for 3 to 4 minutes or until cooked through. Serve with the aïoli.

Note: These cakes are easy to make, and leftovers freeze nicely. If fresh peaches are not yet in season, try apricots for a delicious alternative.

Desserts

Rose Geranium Pound Cake

SERVES 16

10 to 12 fresh rose geranium leaves, cleaned
   and thoroughly dried
3 cups all-purpose flour
1/2 teaspoon salt
1/4 teaspoon baking soda
3 cups (6 sticks) unsalted butter, softened

3 cups Vanilla Rose Geranium Sugar, prepared
   1 week in advance (recipe follows)
6 eggs
1 cup sour cream
2 teaspoons best-quality pure vanilla extract
Confectioners' sugar for sprinkling

EQUIPMENT NEEDED: A stand mixer or an electric hand mixer; a 10-inch tube pan; a wire rack

All ingredients should be at room temperature before beginning this recipe. Grease and flour a 10-inch tube pan. Line the bottom of the pan with the geranium leaves. Mix the flour, salt and baking soda together. Cream the butter and geranium sugar in a mixing bowl of a stand mixer or with an electric hand mixer until light and fluffy. Add two of the eggs and beat well. Add the flour mixture and the remaining four eggs alternately, mixing at low speed after each addition. Stir in the sour cream and vanilla. Spoon into the prepared pan. Place in a cold oven and set the oven temperature to 325 degrees. Bake for 1 1/2 hours or until a cake tester inserted near the center comes out clean. Do not open the oven door during the first hour. Remove from the oven and cool on a wire rack for 15 minutes. Invert onto a serving plate and discard the rose geranium leaves. Let stand until cool.

For presentation, place a paper doily on top of the cake to use as a stencil. Sprinkle with confectioners' sugar and lift up the doily carefully. Place a few rose geranium leaves in a small glass of water to keep the leaves fresh and place the glass in the center hole of the cake.

Note: If fresh rose geranium leaves are not available, try adding a few drops of rose water to the batter.

Vanilla Rose Geranium Sugar

MAKES 3 1/2 CUPS

1 vanilla bean, split lengthwise
3 fresh rose geranium leaves
3 1/2 cups sugar

EQUIPMENT NEEDED: An airtight container

Place the vanilla bean and rose geranium leaves in the sugar in an airtight container and store for 1 week or longer. Remove the vanilla bean and geranium leaves. The result is a perfumed sugar that is delicious when used in baking.

Note: The vanilla bean may be used several times in this way for up to six months.

Scented Geraniums

Known more for their copycat scents than their beauty, scented geraniums add a special fragrance to recipes. Apple, lemon, rose, mint, orange, and pineapple are some of the more than two hundred varieties. Use them to flavor tea, biscuits, cakes, and jellies. Plant geraniums along a path in full sun. When brushed, they will release delicious scents into an herb garden.

Scented geranium (*Pelargonium* spp.)

Basil Orange Truffles

12 ounces good-quality unsweetened chocolate
12 ounces good-quality semisweet chocolate
1 1/4 cups heavy cream
1/2 cup packed fresh basil leaves
3 tablespoons quality orange liqueur, such as
    Grand Marnier

1 tablespoon espresso coffee
Confectioners' sugar or sweet ground chocolate
    for dusting

EQUIPMENT NEEDED: A medium heat-resistant glass bowl; a small saucepan; a fine-meshed sieve; a baking sheet; baking parchment

Shave the chocolate with a serrated knife into a medium heat-resistant glass bowl. Scald the cream in a small saucepan. Remove from the heat and stir in the basil. Let stand, covered, for 20 minutes. Strain the cream through a fine-meshed sieve into a bowl, discarding the basil. Return the infused cream to the saucepan and bring just to a boil. Whisk the cream into the chocolate gradually until the chocolate melts. Whisk in the liqueur and espresso. Chill for 1 to 2 hours or until the chocolate is set. Scoop out the chocolate by rounded teaspoonfuls and shape quickly with cold hands into round but uneven shapes resembling small mushrooms. Roll lightly in confectioners' sugar or ground chocolate and place on a baking sheet lined with baking parchment. Store in the refrigerator and serve at room temperature.

Note: We think we have successfully married herbs to chocolate for this decadent classic. Our version has more chocolate and is denser than other truffles.

Variation: To prepare Lemon Thyme Truffles, substitute the basil and orange liqueur with twenty to twenty-five sprigs of fresh lemon thyme and 3 tablespoons Limoncello liqueur.

Lavender Dates

1 tablespoon lavender buds
8 ounces cream cheese, softened
1 pound pitted fresh dates
Sugar for coating

Chop the lavender buds finely. Combine the lavender and cream cheese in a small bowl and mix well. Slit the dates along one side and stuff with the cream cheese mixture. Roll in sugar to coat.

Note: Beautiful, fast, and easy, these luscious morsels are perfect on a holiday table.

Chocolate Chipotle Brownies

BROWNIES
1/2 cup (1 stick) unsalted butter
4 ounces good-quality unsweetened chocolate
1 cup all-purpose flour
1/4 teaspoon (heaping) cinnamon
4 eggs, at room temperature
1/4 teaspoon salt
2 cups sugar
1/2 teaspoon pure vanilla extract

CHOCOLATE CHIPOTLE FROSTING
6 tablespoons unsalted butter
3 tablespoons good-quality baking cocoa
4 1/2 tablespoons buttermilk
1/8 teaspoon chipotle chili powder
2 to 3 cups confectioners' sugar

EQUIPMENT NEEDED: A double boiler; a stand mixer or an electric hand mixer; a 9×13-inch baking pan; a medium saucepan

To prepare the brownies, preheat the oven to 350 degrees. Melt the butter and chocolate in a double boiler over hot water. Remove from the heat to cool. Sift the flour and cinnamon together. Beat the eggs and salt together in a medium mixing bowl of a stand mixer or with an electric hand mixer until foamy and light in color. Add the sugar and vanilla gradually, beating constantly. Stir in the chocolate mixture by hand. Stir in the flour mixture gently. Pour into a greased 9×13-inch baking pan. Bake for 25 minutes or until the brownies begin to pull away from the sides of the pan.

To prepare the frosting, combine the butter, baking cocoa, buttermilk and chili powder in a medium saucepan. Heat until the butter melts, stirring frequently. Stir in 2 cups of the confectioners' sugar. Add the remaining confectioners' sugar as needed to reach a spreadable consistency. Spread the hot frosting over the hot brownies. Let cool and then cut into bars.

Note: Chili powder in brownies? Yes, and they are delicious.

 ## Cacao
Since Spanish explorers first encountered it in the New World, we have been enjoying the benefits of chocolate products made from seeds of the cacao tree. The Swedish botanist Carl Linnaeus named this very special tree, *Theobroma cacao*, which translated means, "food of the gods." Cacao beans were used by the Aztecs to make a chocolate drink used in rituals and also as currency. European demand for this drink was so great that the French and Spanish established cacao plantations in the Caribbean.

Lemon Mint Squares

1 cup all-purpose flour
1/4 cup confectioners' sugar
1 tablespoon chopped fresh mint leaves
1/2 cup (1 stick) unsalted butter, softened
2 eggs
1 cup granulated sugar
Zest and juice of 1 lemon
1/4 cup all-purpose flour
1/2 teaspoon baking powder
1/4 teaspoon salt
1 teaspoon chopped fresh mint leaves
Confectioners' sugar for sprinkling

EQUIPMENT NEEDED: A 9×9-inch baking pan; an electric hand mixer

Preheat the oven to 350 degrees. Mix 1 cup flour, 1/4 cup confectioners' sugar and 1 tablespoon mint in a small bowl. Add the butter and mix well. Press the dough in a 9×9-inch baking pan. Bake for 15 to 20 minutes or until light golden brown.

Beat the eggs in a medium mixing bowl with an electric hand mixer until eggs are pale yellow. Add the granulated sugar and beat well. Add the lemon zest and lemon juice and mix well. Add 1/4 cup flour, the baking powder, salt and 1 teaspoon mint and mix well. Pour over the hot crust. Bake for 15 to 20 minutes or until set. Remove from oven. Sift confectioners' sugar over the top while hot. Let stand until cool. Cut into 1 1/2-inch squares.

Note: Our version of lemon bars is cool, refreshing, and delightfully minty. For even more mint flavor, add mint as desired to the lemon filling.

Eggs

There is no significant difference in taste between white and brown eggs. White-feathered breeds lay white eggs, and red breeds lay brown eggs. The color of the yolk is determined by the hen's diet and does not indicate freshness. Egg size is determined by the age of the hens laying the eggs: the older the hen, the larger the egg. Always store eggs large side up.

Orange Curry Bars

2 cups all-purpose flour
3/4 teaspoon St. Louis Herb Society
   Curry Powder (page 49) or
   store-bought equivalent
1 cup (2 sticks) butter, softened
1/2 cup confectioners' sugar
Zest of 2 large oranges
4 eggs

2 cups granulated sugar
1/3 cup orange juice concentrate, thawed
1/4 cup all-purpose flour
1 teaspoon baking powder
1 1/2 cups confectioners' sugar
2 1/2 tablespoons butter, softened
2 tablespoons (or more) orange juice
   concentrate, thawed

EQUIPMENT NEEDED: A stand mixer or an electric hand mixer; a 9×13-inch baking pan

Preheat the oven to 350 degrees. Mix 2 cups flour and the curry powder together in a small bowl. Beat 1 cup butter and 1/2 cup confectioners' sugar in a medium bowl of a stand mixer or with an electric hand mixer until light and fluffy. Add the flour mixture and mix well. The dough will be stiff. Press the dough firmly in an ungreased 9×13-inch baking pan. Bake for 15 to 20 minutes or until light golden brown.

Reserve 1/3 teaspoon of the orange zest for the glaze. Beat the eggs in a medium bowl of a stand mixer or with an electric hand mixer until thick and pale yellow. Add 2 cups granulated sugar, the remaining orange zest and 1/3 cup orange juice concentrate and mix well. Stir in 1/4 cup flour and the baking powder. Pour over the hot crust. Return to the oven and bake for 20 to 25 minutes or until golden brown. Remove from the oven to cool.

Mix 1 1/2 cups confectioners' sugar, 2 1/2 tablespoons butter, the reserved 1/3 teaspoon orange zest and 2 tablespoons orange juice concentrate in a small bowl. Add orange juice concentrate if needed to reach a spreadable consistency. Spread over the cooled filling. Chill until the glaze is set. Cut into bars before serving.

Note: Our St. Louis Herb Society Curry Powder gives these orange bars their unique flavor.

Lavender Blossom Tea Cookies

1 cup (2 sticks) unsalted butter, softened
2/3 cup sugar
1 egg, beaten

1^1/4 cups all-purpose flour
3/4 teaspoon baking powder
1 tablespoon lavender buds

EQUIPMENT NEEDED: A stand mixer or an electric hand mixer; a large cookie sheet; baking parchment; a wire rack; an airtight container

Preheat the oven to 350 degrees. Cream the butter and sugar in a medium bowl of a stand mixer or with an electric hand mixer. Add the egg and beat well by hand until light and fluffy. Stir in the flour and baking powder. Add the lavender buds and mix well. Drop by level teaspoonfuls 2 inches apart onto a cookie sheet lined with baking parchment. Bake for 8 to 10 minutes or until pale golden brown and the edges just begin to brown slightly. Watch carefully to prevent overbrowning. Cool on the baking parchment on a wire rack. The cookies will be soft until cooled. Store in an airtight container.

Note: These dainty, wafer-thin cookies are easy to prepare, beautiful, and tempting—a tradition for us to munch on as we work in our St. Louis Herb Society Herb Garden every Tuesday morning.

Lemon Verbena Cookies

4^1/2 cups all-purpose flour
1 teaspoon baking soda
1 teaspoon baking powder
1 cup (2 sticks) butter, softened
1^1/2 cups packed brown sugar

1 egg, beaten
1 cup sour cream
2 teaspoons lemon extract
1/2 cup chopped fresh lemon verbena leaves

EQUIPMENT NEEDED: A stand mixer or an electric hand mixer; a cookie sheet; a wire rack

Preheat the oven to 350 degrees. Mix the flour, baking soda and baking powder together. Cream the butter and brown sugar in the bowl of a stand mixer or with an electric hand mixer until light and fluffy. Add the egg, sour cream and lemon extract and mix well. Add the flour mixture gradually, mixing well after each addition. Fold in the lemon verbena. Drop by teaspoonfuls onto a greased cookie sheet. Bake for 10 minutes. Cool on a wire rack.

 Edible Flowers

Flower cookery has been around since Roman times and was popular in the Victorian era. Today, edible flowers are used in many cuisines. When using edible flowers in recipes or as a garnish, keep it simple in both appearance and flavor. The dish should not be overpowered with perfume. Do not use flowers that have been exposed to pesticides or herbicides, so avoid using flowers from florists or nurseries. Always wash before using.

Orange Basil Sandwich Cookies

1 cup (2 sticks) unsalted butter, softened
3/4 cup sugar
2 1/2 teaspoons chopped fresh basil leaves
Zest of 1 large orange
1/2 teaspoon baking powder

2 1/4 cups all-purpose flour
Sugar for dipping
1/2 cup cream cheese, softened
1/3 cup orange marmalade

EQUIPMENT NEEDED: An electric hand mixer; a large cookie sheet; baking parchment; a wire rack; an airtight container

Preheat the oven to 400 degrees. Beat the butter at medium speed in a mixing bowl with an electric hand mixer for 40 seconds. Add 3/4 cup sugar, the basil, orange zest and baking powder and beat well. Beat in enough of the flour to form a stiff dough. Stir in any of the remaining flour by hand.

Shape the dough into 1-inch balls. Place 2 inches apart on a cookie sheet lined with baking parchment. Flatten the balls to 1/2 inch thick with the bottom of a glass dipped in sugar. Bake for 5 to 8 minutes or until light brown on the bottom. Cool on the cookie sheet for 1 minute. Remove to a wire rack to cool completely.

Combine the cream cheese and orange marmalade in a small bowl and mix well. Spread on the flat side of one-half of the cookies. Top with the remaining cookies flat side down. Serve immediately or store in an airtight container in the refrigerator, separating each layer of cookies with waxed paper. Let stand at room temperature for 1 hour before serving.

Note: These lovely cookies take a bit longer to make than ordinary cookies but are well worth it. Little flecks of basil make them as pretty as they are delicious.

Chai Meringues

1/2 teaspoon ground cardamom
1/2 teaspoon cinnamon
1/4 teaspoon ground cloves
1/8 teaspoon freshly grated nutmeg

Pinch of freshly ground pepper
3 egg whites, at room temperature
1 cup sugar

EQUIPMENT NEEDED: An electric hand mixer; a large cookie sheet; baking parchment; an airtight container

Preheat the oven to 250 degrees. Mix the cardamom, cinnamon, cloves, nutmeg and pepper in a small bowl. Beat the egg whites at low speed with an electric hand mixer in a medium bowl until foamy. Add the sugar gradually, beating at high speed until shiny, stiff peaks form. Add the spice mixture and beat just enough to distribute evenly. Drop by teaspoonfuls into small mounds on a cookie sheet lined with baking parchment.

Bake for 1 1/2 hours. Turn off the oven and do not open the oven door. Let the meringues stand in the oven for 3 to 10 hours to dry. Store in an airtight container.

Note: These light and delicate beauties are best when made on a dry, nonhumid day.

Cranberry Rosemary Meringue Pie

1³/4 cups sugar
³/4 cup water
4 cups fresh or frozen cranberries
Zest of 1 large orange
1/2 teaspoon finely chopped fresh rosemary
1/4 teaspoon ground mace
1 tablespoon all-purpose flour
1 tablespoon cornstarch

1 tablespoon water
4 egg yolks
2 tablespoons salted butter
1 baked (9-inch) deep-dish pie shell
4 egg whites, at room temperature
1/2 cup sugar
1/2 teaspoon (scant) orange extract (optional)

EQUIPMENT NEEDED: A medium saucepan; an electric hand mixer

Combine 1³/4 cups sugar and ³/4 cup water in a medium saucepan. Cook over medium heat to form a simple syrup. Add the cranberries. Cook until the cranberries pop. Remove from the heat. Stir in the orange zest, rosemary and mace. Let stand to cool slightly.

Mix the flour, cornstarch and 1 tablespoon water in a small bowl until smooth. Whisk in the eggs yolks until smooth. Add about 1/4 cup of the cranberry mixture and mix well. Stir into the remaining cranberry mixture in the saucepan. Return to a boil. Reduce the heat and simmer for 3 minutes or until the mixture thickens to a pudding consistency. Remove from the heat. Add the butter and stir until melted. Pour into the baked pie shell.

Beat the egg whites in a medium bowl at high speed with an electric hand mixer until soft peaks form. Add 1/2 cup sugar and the orange extract gradually, beating until stiff peaks form.

Preheat the oven to 325 degrees. Place a heart-shaped, star-shaped or other desired-shaped cookie cutter in the center of the pie. Spread the meringue over the top of the pie and around the sides of the cookie cutter. Remove the cookie cutter to reveal a decorative red shape in the center. Bake for 15 minutes or until the meringue begins to turn golden brown.

Note: A very pretty pie perfect for holidays, especially Valentine's Day.

Bosc Pear Pie

1 (2-crust) pie pastry
4 Bosc pears, peeled and thinly sliced
1 tart apple, such as Granny Smith, peeled and thinly sliced
1 teaspoon fresh lemon juice
1/4 cup honey
2 tablespoons brandy
1/3 cup packed brown sugar
1/4 teaspoon cinnamon
1/4 teaspoon ground cloves
1/4 teaspoon ginger
1/4 teaspoon ground mace
1 1/2 tablespoons cornstarch
1 tablespoon butter, cut into small cubes
Egg wash for brushing
1 cup caramel sauce
1 tablespoon brandy

EQUIPMENT NEEDED: A 9-inch pie plate

Preheat the oven to 375 degrees. Line a 9-inch pie plate with one of the pie pastries. Chill in the refrigerator.

Combine the pears and apple in a large bowl. Add the lemon juice, honey and 2 tablespoons brandy and mix well. Mix the brown sugar, cinnamon, cloves, ginger, mace and cornstarch in a small bowl. Sprinkle over the pear mixture and toss to combine. Spoon into the pastry-lined pie plate. Dot with the butter. Prick the remaining pie pastry in several places for ventilation or use small cookie cutters to cut designs in the pastry. Place over the top of the pie, sealing and fluting the edge. Brush with egg wash. Bake for 40 to 50 minutes or until the crust is golden brown and the filling is bubbling through the vents.

Mix the caramel sauce with 1 tablespoon brandy in a small bowl. Serve with the pie.

Note: The combination of pears, apples, and brandy is what makes this pie so good.

Blackberry Basil Tart with Mascarpone Lemon Cream

1 cup all-purpose flour
2 tablespoons sugar
1/2 cup (1 stick) salted butter, softened
1 tablespoon white vinegar
3 cups fresh blackberries
1 cup sugar
2 1/2 tablespoons all-purpose flour
3 tablespoons chopped fresh basil leaves

1/2 cup heavy whipping cream
8 ounces mascarpone cheese,
   at room temperature
2 teaspoons fresh lemon juice
1/2 teaspoon pure vanilla extract
Fresh blackberries or blackberry jam
   for garnish
Sprig of fresh basil leaves for garnish

EQUIPMENT NEEDED: A 10-inch tart pan with removable bottom; an electric hand mixer

Spray the bottom of a 10-inch tart pan with a removable bottom with nonstick cooking spray. Mix 1 cup flour and 2 tablespoons sugar in a bowl. Cut in the butter with your fingers or a fork until crumbly. Add the vinegar and mix well. Press the dough evenly over the bottom and up the side of the prepared tart pan. Press a straight-sided measuring cup against the bottom edge to ensure a uniform thickness. Chill for 15 minutes.

Preheat the oven to 400 degrees. Combine 3 cups blackberries, 1 cup sugar, 2 1/2 tablespoons flour and 3 tablespoons basil in a medium bowl and stir gently. Spoon into the pastry-lined tart pan. Bake for 40 to 50 minutes or until the crust is golden brown and the filling is bubbly. Remove from the oven to cool.

Whip the whipping cream with an electric hand mixer in a mixing bowl until soft peaks form. Add the cheese, lemon juice and vanilla and beat until stiff. Spread carefully over the filling, beginning with the edge and ending in the center. Garnish with fresh blackberries or blackberry jam in a decorative design over the top. Garnish with a sprig of basil leaves.

Note: You will look forward to blackberry season so that you can make this fabulous tart, and it has a crust that is one of our favorites.

Lemon Verbena Charlotte

SERVES 8 TO 10

6 egg yolks
3/4 cup sugar
Juice and zest of 2 lemons
1 envelope unflavored gelatin
1/2 cup packed fresh lemon verbena leaves,
   coarsely chopped

1 cup boiling water
6 egg whites, at room temperature
3/4 cup sugar
2 packages ladyfingers, split
1/2 cup heavy whipping cream, whipped
Fresh lemon verbena leaves for garnish

EQUIPMENT NEEDED: A double boiler; a small saucepan with a lid; a fine-meshed sieve or paper coffee filter; an electric hand mixer; a 9-inch springform pan

Combine the egg yolks, 3/4 cup sugar, the lemon juice and lemon zest in a double boiler. Cook over simmering water until thickened, stirring constantly. Remove from the heat to cool.

Soften the gelatin in a small amount of cold water in a small bowl. Place 1/2 cup lemon verbena leaves in a small saucepan and cover with the boiling water. Steep, covered, for 5 minutes. Strain through a fine-meshed sieve or paper coffee filter into a glass measure, making sure the infusion measures a scant 1 cup. Return the infusion to the saucepan. Return to a boil; remove from the heat. Add the softened gelatin and stir to dissolve. Let stand until cool. Add to the egg yolk mixture and mix well.

Beat the egg whites in a large mixing bowl with an electric hand mixer at high speed until soft peaks form. Add 3/4 cup sugar gradually, beating until stiff, glossy peaks form. Fold into the egg yolk mixture.

Line the bottom and side of a greased 9-inch springform pan with the ladyfingers, split side in. Pour the egg mixture into the prepared pan. Chill, covered, for 8 to 10 hours.

To serve, run a knife around the edge of the pan to loosen the charlotte from the side. Remove the side of the pan. Spread the whipped cream over the top. Garnish with lemon verbena leaves.

Note: If you are concerned about using raw egg whites, use whites from eggs pasteurized in their shells, or use an equivalent amount of meringue powder and follow the package directions.

St. Louis Herb Society

161

Fruit on Lemon Grass Skewers with Orange Tarragon Sauce

4 lemon grass stalks
8 cups assorted seasonal fruit, such as melons,
   strawberries, bananas, mangoes and pineapples,
   cut into chunks
1 tablespoon chopped fresh stevia leaves
Chopped fresh tarragon, mint or lemon verbena leaves for garnish
Orange Tarragon Sauce (page 163)

Peel the dry outer leaves from the lemon grass to reveal the inner core. Cut each stalk into halves lengthwise to resemble a skewer and make a point at the narrow end. Combine the fruit and stevia in a large bowl and toss to mix. Thread the fruit onto the lemon grass skewers. Garnish with tarragon. Serve with Orange Tarragon Sauce.

Note: Stevia provides just a hint of sweetness without sugar, and lemon grass makes a beautiful presentation for this light dessert, perfect for entertaining on warm summer evenings. Stevia has been grown for centuries for its properties as a sugar substitute, and when processed it is thirty times stronger than sugar.

Variation: Serve the fruit in goblets topped with Orange Tarragon Sauce and garnished with fresh tarragon.

Orange Tarragon Sauce

MAKES ABOUT 1¹/₂ CUPS

8 ounces cream cheese, softened
¹/₂ cup confectioners' sugar
³/₄ cup sour cream
¹/₃ cup heavy whipping cream
2 tablespoons (or more) Cointreau, or other orange liqueur
2 teaspoons chopped fresh tarragon
Zest of 1 orange

EQUIPMENT NEEDED: A food processor

Process the cream cheese, confectioners' sugar, sour cream, whipping cream, 2 tablespoons liqueur, the tarragon and orange zest in a food processor until smooth. Add additional Cointreau to taste. Spoon into a serving bowl. Chill, covered, for 4 to 10 hours before serving.

Variation: For Lemon Verbena Sauce, use fresh lemon verbena leaves and lemon zest instead of the tarragon and orange zest.

Lavender or Mint Sorbet

2 cups water
1 cup sugar
1/2 cup sprigs of fresh lavender or sprigs of fresh mint
1/2 cup fresh lemon juice

EQUIPMENT NEEDED: A noncorrosive saucepan; a sieve; an ice cream or sorbet freezer

Bring the water and sugar to a boil in a noncorrosive saucepan. Add the lavender. Simmer, covered, for 15 to 20 minutes. Remove from the heat. Strain the mixture through a sieve into a bowl, discarding the solids. Let stand until cool. Stir the lemon juice into the cooled syrup. Pour into an ice cream or sorbet freezer container. Freeze using the manufacturer's directions.

Note: The sorbet can be frozen in a shallow freezer-proof dish or ice cube tray. For a smoother sorbet, stir the mixture several times during the freezing process.

Variation: For Rosemary Sorbet, substitute rosemary for the lavender and 1/4 cup dry white wine for one-half of the lemon juice.

 ## Chocolate Sorbet Cups

Melt one cup (six ounces) semisweet chocolate chips and two tablespoons butter together. Using a pastry brush, brush a fairly thick coating of the chocolate mixture on the side and bottom of small fluted paper baking cups. Freeze until firm. Carefully peel off the paper. Place a mint leaf in the bottom of each cup before filling with a scoop of Mint Sorbet (above).

Vanilla Bean Ice Cream with Lavender Syrup

1 cup honey
3/4 cup water
1/3 cup organically grown lavender leaves
Premium-quality vanilla bean ice cream
Lavender leaves or lavender buds for garnish

EQUIPMENT NEEDED: A small saucepan; a candy thermometer; a sieve; a sterilized small canning jar with a lid

Combine the honey, water and 1/3 cup lavender leaves in a small saucepan. Cook to 190 degrees on a candy thermometer. Remove immediately from the heat so the honey does not burn. Strain through a sieve into a sterilized small canning jar and tightly seal, discarding the solids. Store until ready to serve.

Serve over vanilla bean ice cream and garnish with lavender.

Note: Experiment with other herbs, such as lemon balm, lemon verbena, lemon thyme, rosemary, or basil. Just be certain they have been organically grown.

Lavender (*Lavandula angustifolia*)

The St. Louis Herb Society

Toni Ansboro	Glenda Finnie	Diane Kohl	Barbara Rezny
Margery Armstrong	Barbara Finbloom	Nancy LaBrier	Ruth Masterson Ripa
Barbara Barr	Elaine Flieg	Marcia LaCour-Little	David Sacks
Jean Beck	Pam Foster	Pat Leigh	Jane Saghir
Paulette Bliss	Katie Garner	Tracie Lewis	Nancy Schiller
Judy Bolian	Betsy Gee	Connie Lippert	Beverly Schmitt
Nancy Bridwell	Kerry Goldstein	Nadine Mahe	Pat Schutte
Peggy Burris	Betty Guarraia	Kathy Marks-Petetit	Joy Stinger
Eileen Carr	Mary Hammer	Audrey Mathews	Lee Street
Ann Case	Gwen Hardin	Katie McGuigan	Suzanne Switzer
Audrey Claus	Judith Harmon	Sue McNamara	Nancy Thompson
Ruth Cobb	Monica Hartenstine	Joan Meyer	Carol Tischer
Ruth Conway	Linda Hensley	Karen Smead Mondale	Candace Ulrich
Anne Schlafly Cori	Jan Hermann	Joyce Niewoehner	Dreanna Vallina
Phyllis Dixon	Carol Higgins	Jeanne Nowicke	JoAnn Rivinus Vorih
Suzanne Dorris	Sheila Hoffmeister	Barbara O'Brien	Linn Wells
Sharon Dougherty	Mary Ann Hogan	Barbara Ottolini	Mary Clair Wenger
Joyce Driemeyer	Mary Holekamp	Elisabeth Ottolini	Linda Whitten
Sondra Ellis	Patricia Holt	Sue Palmer	Joan Williams
Dorothy Ernst	LaVerne Jaudes	Sharon Platt	Carolyn Willmore
Melanie Fathman	Kim Joern	Kim Pope	Marian Wuest
Kathleen Ferrell	Nancy Kirchhoff	Estelle Powers	Marjorie Young
Dorothy Feutz	Lynn Kiske	Stephanie Prade	
Abigail Filippello	Carroll Kohl	Sue Reed	

Index

To order additional copies of

Herbal Cookery

please contact us at our Web site
www.stlouisherbsociety.org